Against Black People

The European Will to Conquer

Brian C. McGuire

Against Black People
The European Will To Conquer

Against Black People
The European Will To Conquer
Copyright 2022 - Brian C. McGuire
Library of Congress 1-11212581451

ISBN: 13: 979-8425040169
IMPRINT: Indie Publishing

Printed in the United States of America
10 9 8 7 6 5 4 3 2 1

Against Black People
The European Will To Conquer

by
Brian C. McGuire
Towson University

FAR-LEFT PUBLICATIONS

Brian C. McGuire

Against Black People
The European Will To Conquer

Brian C. McGuire was born in Baltimore, Maryland on May 31, 1970. He spent thirteen years serving in the United States Armed Forces. He received a Bachelor of Science from Towson University. His areas of research interest include the mental terrain of Community Psychology: A field of Human Services that places special emphasis on problems associated with urban groups and how they adapt under low socioeconomic conditions during childhood, adolescence, and throughout the course of adult development and aging, and sociocultural influences (including theoretical concepts pertaining to how various dimensions of culture influence stress and coping). Brian is also the author of five exceptional indie reference books to include Refusing to Learn: Really, How Dumb Do You Think I Am, and Racism: In the Behavioral Context of Intergroup Conflict and Hostility.

TABLE OF CONTENTS

Dedication

Against Black People: The European Will to Conquer is dedicated to Blacks who refuse to conform to Western expectations. May the pages of this book comfort you in your fight for freedom.

McGuire, 2022

Acknowledgements

The concept for writing this book began in the year 2021. Amid a multitude of discussions on race, ethnicity, and culture, it became increasingly clear that Western civilization wants to return to an earlier and generally worse state of existence. Although some people would say the idea of westerners wanting to regress back to a state of segregation is a stretch from reinstituting chattel slavery, others would disagree. Having addressed this topic in the past with increasing interest from young White Americans, I felt it was time to create a reference book, one that examined the motivation behind Europeans and their desire for global conquest.

In this book, I attempt to show that the world is conforming to Western expectations. As such, it is becoming increasingly dependent on Western civilizations to survive. The problem is Western governments are abusing the world's natural resources. At the current rate of progression, the world will suffer tremendous loss. A loss of health, wealth, and dignity, humans are destroying the planet and at what cost? I believe humans will destroy more than the world itself. We are now at the brink of losing our humanity.

Although this book has not undergone an advisory board to better corroborate the facts, a team of editors have given their time and effort to ensure that the materials covered in this book are written with regard to accepted standards of correctness. And for that reason, I thank each one of them.

As always, I am grateful to Yvonne M. Drake who continues to suffer through my research. She has been my eyes and ears throughout most of my journey. I'd like to give a personal thanks to her for always being present throughout the writing process of my books. Her love and encouragement inspire my confidence. It carries me during my most doubtful or darkest moments.

I am glad to announce the return of Anita L. Opher. She is the primary editor for most of my writing projects. Without her brilliance and editing genius, many of my books would not exist. Needless to say, she is deeply appreciated. Thanks for hanging in there with me.

I'd also like to thank Kendra Rhodes for her courageous commitment to the editing of this book. Somehow, she always manages to find time during her busy work schedule to review and edit a few chapters of my manuscripts. She's a great inspiration to me. What a champ!

Their professionalism is greatly appreciated.

Prologue
On Against Black People

What I find to be most exciting yet troubling is writing on the topic of racism. It is of profound importance to me. Racism has consumed most of the planet. In fact, nearly every aspect of human behavior is governed by racism. It is so impactful one can even say racism is a part of human behavior be the determinate nature or nurture. It's definitely part of the human condition, dating back to biblical times.

I often become excited whenever I uncover information that breaks through the complex and entangled surface of racism, information that yields even the slightest glimpse of intricacy lying just beneath. Racism entangles the facts with value judgments. As a result, it is hard to determine the worth, appropriateness, or importance of people. Much like racism, value judgment is based on personal beliefs, opinions, or prejudices rather than facts. Therefore, it is indicative of your more pervasive –isms to include sexism, conservatism, even communism. Value judgments are inextricably linked to racism. Now, isn't that enough to stimulate your intellectual processes? Investigating widespread problems may not be as physically exciting as winning a battle in the Ultimate Fighting Championship (UFC), but finding solutions to world problems can be every bit as stimulating.

Whenever possible, I try to explain certain comparative assumptions between European behavior and racial aggression in everyday settings, a challenge that will add excitement and beauty to your voyages of discovery. As a scholar, I have an obligation to share my knowledge in a way that gives clarifying information to interested parties, communities, cultures, and ethnic groups. It is also my duty to avoid the temptation of influencing readers and resist trying to change perspectives I am not invited to change.

As a researcher, I have an obligation to write in a nonjudgmental way that does not favor or discriminate against any particular group. Therefore, the purpose of this prologue is to explain some of the intellectual challenges that guide my research and, perhaps, the nature of certain topics that make this book possible.

One of my main objectives was to present concepts in a way that would be mentally rigorous and intellectually stimulating. When developing any of my books, one of the major challenges I confront is how to cover a broad volume of information at the risk of giving attention to only the obvious. My personal bias is against the textbook approach. I believe that textbooks do not enable readers to gain critical knowledge of concepts more than familiarizing them with superficial ideas, thus losing them in a vast sea of information. That's why, in this book, I try to identify the most important similarities between European behavior and racial aggression while presenting it in-depth rather than giving superficial knowledge of the topic.

One example of this method is in my treatment of the introduction. The introduction provides a framework for what's to come. It is intended to help the reader think critically about later discussions by adding context to the current set of concepts. Therefore, I try to eliminate the dangers of superficiality by encouraging readers to think critically throughout this book rather than take a shallow approach to familiarizing themselves with surface issues. In subsequent chapters, I continue this method by discussing topics in-depth where needed, giving brief summaries on related topics.

Chapter 1, The European Will to Conquer, begins with a biblical passage that, when translated, tells the reader what led to European conquest. I also give an overview of European history and which influences were able to affect their thinking or actions. I discuss their motivation in various regards throughout the book. Racism and pride are rooted in the prehistoric sources of European aggression, which describes the motivation behind their will to conquer. In chapter 2, The Context of European Aggression, I use a few approaches to understanding European behavior, specifically the motivation behind European aggression and its impact on nonwhites. I also consider an older approach to understanding the importance of using race as a marker for determining groups of humans. Chapter 3 discusses the motivation behind Western technology. Important concepts about aggression are introduced here. Readers will learn that technology is an expression of Western aggression. It is also the behavioral attitude of a society that determines the type of technology to be developed. Later in this chapter and throughout others, we discuss whether technology is needed to develop civilization or is even necessary to advance civilization.

Chapter 4 describes Europeans and their tendency to develop racism. We look at the motivation behind it. We also take an in-depth look at European progress and the assertion of White supremacy. We discuss the topic of value judgment in chapter 5. We take a look at why the United States refuses to hold other countries in high regard in terms of personal standards or priorities. Then in chapter

6, we discuss Europeans and their willingness to embrace racism. This chapter is an in-depth discussion on their stubborn persistence to resists change. In chapter 7, we looked at the violence of intellectual paroxysm. It deals with the internal conflict that exists well within the White race. Many scholars believe that the level of aggression we see in White people today is a result of a complex (a disease of the mind) that causes outbursts of violence. An example of this intellectual disease is the belief in one's own superiority. Last, in chapter 8, we talk about the concept of race. Here, I try to prove that regardless of its social uses, race is a valid concept. Such as, I point to its roots to support the notion that race is a biological construct. In the end, I provide evidence that supports the notion that race is a biological concept.

In the first half of this prologue, we gave a few reasons why I find racism to be an exciting topic of discussion. We also talked about the excitement of making breakthroughs on the topic and finding important discoveries that connect racism to pervasive systems, states, or conditions. Next, in the introduction, we will give you a quick look at the theme, revealing important discoveries that connect racism to a belief that drives the European will to conquer.

Introduction
Against Black People

What doesn't kill you makes you stronger.

Friedrich Nietzsche (1844 – 1900)

What doesn't kill you makes you stronger. Friedrich Nietzsche (1844 – 1900) wrote that famous aphorism as an affirmation of resilience. Black Americans are a resilient people. They've shown the ability to recover quickly from setbacks that affects the nature of their situation.

For example, how do a people whose grim lives are so full of trauma influence the course of twentieth century history? Black people turned their struggle or the Black experience into a rich history that had a profound impact on Western civilization. People like James Baldwin turned his poverty and trauma into a rich literary harvest that impacted the minds of countless millions. The adaptive behaviors of Blacks help to reduce the real social dangers of interacting with Whites. It also helps to bring balance to a world where it is or, at least, seems to be in imminent danger of losing its humanity.

Whites and Blacks are most certainly in conflict against one another. The opposition or conflict existing between them creates real social problems that ultimately impact people from every walk of life: choosing sides, for example or having to make a decision to profit from those considered exploitable as a way to gain in success.

This introduction is an explanatory section that summarizes the nature of this book. As a scholar, I have carefully evaluated the benefits of sharing this information with you. Any oversights, especially mistakes made on historical grounds, could lead to incorrect assumptions about the relationships of power that exist between Whites and Blacks, specifically the wanton violence "against Black people." What you may not know is the goal or purpose of this book is to reflect on the struggles that exist between two separate and distinct cultural systems. So, prepare yourselves. This book is going to be every bit as exciting and challenging as competing in a downhill slalom.

Against Black People

Against Black People: The European Will to Conquer will not resolve every knotty problem akin to Blacks. No, it doesn't give us firmness of mind or a sense of purpose. But it does give us insight into the nature of a complex people: Who they are, what makes them the way they are, why they think and act the way they do, and how we can better interact with them given a careful evaluation of our situation. I am enthusiastic about this book's potential to improve on your understanding of life as we continue steadily through the twenty-first century. It is an exciting time to dawn new discoveries about the thinking strategies of Europeans and, quite possibly, ourselves as we learn to socially interact with one another in the real world.

To an extent, what we find in the pages of this book might cause you to feel uneasy. I have a talent for finding answers to complex problems most researchers fail to consider. For example, it may not seem like Western technology is the main problem source for humanity. After all, Western civilization is the leading source of production on the planet. But what you may not know is Western technology is an expression of European aggression. As you can tell, I make every possible effort to uncover the truth about human nature, even the unspoken truth. If you don't already know, this book is filled with rigorous research that will turn up the unexpected.

Now, I must tell you that Against Black People: The European Will to Conquer is not for the faint of heart. What we discuss in the pages of this book is critical. I must also tell you that the world is against Black people, negative antiblack sentiments felt by entire races. Curiously, I am not alone in the thoughts or ideas I share with you today. Therefore, the information provided in this book may appear awkward or untrue for some people. But the sentiments felt will appeal to most of you.

Granted, this book is not about sharing awkward feelings of sentiments but the actual factuals of widespread problems prevailing among Black people. And while it may seem personal for me, I am not obsessively anxious about White people and their thoughts or motives. Nor do I have any reason to take selfish or unfair advantage of a people or their situation in order to gain in benefits. Against Black People: the European Will to Conquer is written to serve as a candid public discourse against those who engage in overt racist behavior.

Racism is defined by White supremacy. And White supremacy contributes to some of the most difficult and defining moments in history to which I speak. It is my hope that by the end of this book, readers will come to consider, as I have, Black people are not the main problem source in the world. In fact, they never were.

Some people will say this book is Afrocentric. In this way, I've come to realize that there is no way to make my findings more appealing or flattering to critics. So, I will be candid in a way that they find either refreshing or distasteful.

It is my belief that the problem with the world today, as it was then, is White supremacy. That being said, I will attempt to show you that the world is conforming to Western expectations. As such, it is becoming increasingly dependent on Western civilizations to survive. What this means is developing countries are modeling behind their Western counterparts. Besides war, pollution, and resource rape, imitating Western countries appears to be endangering our humanity.

Many countries are developing a lack of compassion for others. Countries like Columbia in South America are causing many of its citizens to suffer needlessly. Many of its Afro-Latino population have been displaced from their homes. Turned loose on the streets of Columbia, most of them have migrated to the United States in search of refuge. Other developing countries are experiencing similar problems.

Many developing countries can be seen imitating Western countries. Western ways of behaving, their style of dress, lifestyle choices, and other expressions considered Western, at present, contributes to their exaggerated sense of confidence or pride. The problem is many citizens in developing countries learn to look down on nonwhites just like their Western counterparts. Racial abuse, official murders, and the cruel act of racism are consuming most developing countries. At their current rate of bigotry, the world will suffer tremendous loss. What will be lost is far more detrimental than destroying the planet?

We are now at the brink of losing our humanity. Let those of you who agree with my findings and support the research bring truth to bear. As broad-minded people free from prejudice and open to change, you are the basis for which humanity exists. Now, that doesn't mean I've written this book to offend the fragile sensibilities of White people. We each share in the qualities of life characteristic of humans as a whole. It is my hope that this book will remind readers to have kindness or compassion for others.

A Shift in Racial Dynamics

The problem is the world has experienced dynamic changes in role reversal. The result is these changes turned an entire world against Black people. In fact, it's been recorded, chronologically, throughout the course of world history. Starting with the destruction of Black civilizations in Africa and the Moors' expulsion from early Spain, to the African slave trade in the Americas, the relationships of power existing between Whites and Blacks shifted, changing the dynamics of their existence. Today, Blacks have been psychologically duped by the very people they westernized or civilized. And for centuries, Whites taught Blacks to believe they are ungrateful wretches for not conforming to Western expectations.

People forced to exist in a less healthy or, generally, in a worse state have more problems than usual. Their problems have such a profound impact on them that it is a constant threat to their survival. Truth of the matter is racial oppression is a particular problem of White people. Their morals, values, and psychology more often work to reduce Blacks to an undesirable state.

It is not enough for Whites to rob Blacks of their identity, strip them of their dignity, and then deny them their humanity. No, Whites have to teach Blacks that Europeans are the basis of life and through their will Blacks will learn to live. Fortunately for Black people, there's been an awakening taking place over the course of decades, perhaps the last century even. Blacks are fighting to take back what is unlawfully permitted by their oppressors.

In this book, I try to uncover some of the most horrid yet fascinating aspects of the human condition. I will also attempt to show that race is not only a natural concept, it is a necessary marker for categorizing people. I will further attempt to show that racism is a condition that affects the humanity of not only one race but, specifically, the White race. Here, I hope to prove that Whites are still evolving and therefore not pure Homo sapiens (i.e., Homo sapien, sapien).

What evidence do I present as the basis for my arguments, my claims? Today's Europeans or the White race has origins rooted in the prehistoric development of Europe. The first signs of Europeans or early modern Europeans date back from about 50 thousand to 30 thousand years B.C. Early modern Europeans, or Cro-

Magnon, lacked the humanity characteristic of Homo sapien, sapien. In the same regard, modern-day Europeans or the White race lack in kindness or compassion for others. I provide evidence for the aforementioned and more throughout the course of this book.

My Intentions for the Reader

My intention is to help the reader understand the conspiracy behind controlling or oppressing Black people. Along the way, we will consider the possibility that America is moving in a contrary direction. Many Americans are opposing their inherent American values. I say inherent values because America's initial values centers on the pursuit of personal happiness and independence rather than striving to attain collective goals or interests. Today, Americans are at odds with deciding on whether the country should continue in its earlier beliefs.

Questioning Heritage

The ultimate goal of America's forefathers was grounded in the early belief that American society existed for the benefit of White people. It did not include Black folk, just the colonial members who founded the country. They refused to be constrained by an aristocracy or any social class holding hereditary titles or offices where the power is wielded by the nobility. They strongly believed that such governmental systems prevented ordinary people from becoming successful. The result of establishing an aristocracy meant many people would suffer great indignities. So, with the formation of a bureaucracy, those who were commonplace in England would have a chance to ascend to the status of nobility or the highest social class in American society.

The problem with forming a new governmental system in America was that politicians facilitated, not in the idea of making the most important decisions at the state level, which is the basis of a bureaucracy, but placed power into hands of a small group of elites who would eventually control the nation's institutions. Today, the cultural elite are of the highest social class in American society. It is their belief in superiority that convinces White people they have the right to disadvantage others. Even members of the same race are often disadvantaged under this system of White privilege.

The social and cultural barriers in place today, the ones that are supposed to place Whites in a favorable position relative to others, prevents many of them from competing for a fair share of the profits, benefits and, ultimately, power. Yet, America was founded on the very principles of freedom or liberty and justice for all. The irony is that the cultural elite or the White establishment refuse to share power with commonplace White folk and oppressed sects of government. Their elite position or status in politics and society enables them to form an American aristocracy. If that much is true, then the question we need to ask ourselves is for whom was this country intended? What did the founding fathers mean when they wrote the US Constitution?

The US Constitution was written with the intended purpose of raising the sociopolitical status of the founding members of American society and their plutocrat offspring, not commonplace White folk. It also excludes Black folk from receiving certain rights, entitlements, and privileges, a system of advantage that has been in place since its adoption in 1789. Further, nonwhites have been persecuted under the basic laws or principles by which America is governed. In this way, we need to look at the mindset or motivation that determines the behavioral outlook of people. We especially need to consider people who conspire to control or oppress Blacks ultimately for profit. Here, we can look at the violence that gives special insight to the nature of Europeans and their will to conquer.

As we will see in upcoming chapters, more than situational factors are involved in the evolution of Europeans. Entire social systems bring about change-producing forces that offset the circle of life. These forces are continuously used by Europeans to exploit, oppress, and humiliate Black people. Such maltreatment often occurs without provocation. In chapter 1 and throughout the remainder of this book, I hope to tease apart the precise links that connect racism to the European will to conquer. Simply said, I would like to find out what motivates White behavior. I mean, what makes them tick?

Chapter 1
The European Will to Conquer

Rebuke the beast among the reeds, the herd of bulls among the calves of the nations. Humbled, may the beast bring bars of silver. Scatter the nations who delight in war.

The King James Version Holy Bible (Psalm 68:30)

Psalm 68:30 has several meanings we can readily apply to this chapter. Here, I offer a translation and connections to help you better understand the European struggle for independence from the Muslim world. Notice that Psalm 68:30 is a message to any nation of people who are fighting for freedom against the tyranny of oppression. When literally translated, Psalm 68:30 highlights the significance of Spain's struggle for independence from the Moors. Pay very close attention to the symbolisms from the passage.

The opening passage in Psalm 68:30, rebuke the beast among the reeds, tells you to reprimand or criticize the Moors for their shortcomings. While the Moors were brilliant educators of the arts and sciences, it became increasingly dangerous to interact with them. Due to their aggressiveness, they were likely to inflict harm or injury on people, much like a wild beast, hence the need to rebuke the Moors presence in Europe.

Reeds are tall water plants. The Moors were said to traveled from the sea of reeds. So, Psalms 68:30 is, perhaps, a warning to the people of Europe. The Moors were considered large Black and fearsome men who constantly traveled the world in search of conquest. They often traveled in large armadas on the open sea and armies on land. Their military presence was often referred to as a herd of bulls by Europeans; hence, the term beast was used in fear to describe the Moors.

Next is the phrase, "may the beast bring bars of silver." Bars of silver have two meanings. First, silver was the currency-base used to pay educators. It also referred to the level of science the Moors were willing to teach Europeans, a level of knowledge that enlighten Europeans from their failure to understand their own ignorance, prejudice, and superstitions. Their mentality ultimately led the Moors to believe Europeans were a child race. Therefore, Europe housed nations of children, hence use of the term calves of nations.

The Moors were a military society that found delight in fighting wars. They civilized much of Spain through continuous conquest. The Moors were expelled (scattered) from Spain due to their lack of respect (delight in war) for the Spanish people. White people have been conspiring against Black people ever since Europeans secretly planned to expel the Moors from Europe. In all fairness, the Moors did Westernize Europe by enlightening the cultural attitudes of its citizens. They taught art, science, culture, and other manifestations of the human intellectual achievement to Europeans, ending the Dark-Age.

For any readers who just missed my subtle hints (i.e., the relationship between Black people and the Moors),

I will be clear and concise from this point forward. The English translation of the word Moor is Black. It is a derivative of the Roman or Greek root Moorish which, when literately translated, means "the Blacks." Also, in this moment of clarity, I must say that the Moors were Arabians which, in part, made up Muslim people, their culture, and their countries, collectively, but not their racial identity. The racial identity of the Moors was, in fact, Africoid (Black). As for their religion, the Moors made up, primarily, the Islamic faith.

Understanding what we've learned so far, the first set of questions is easy to reason. "How did the Moors get pushed out of Europe? Specifically, why were they expelled?" We do know they were among the world's greatest conquerors, which leads to the next set of questions. "What happened to the Moors? And, where are they today?" We will answer each of these questions shortly. But, before we delve into this next experience, allow me to digress.

This chapter is a bit of a digression from the central topic. But, I find it helpful to give you the necessary information to align yourself with my line of argument. Most of the information found in this chapter is taken from European literature. But, I have confidence in the way the material is presented.

Now, in the opening passage of this chapter, I gave you a full translation of Psalm 68:30. It should give you insight into the internal struggle that existed between

Europeans and the Moors. Next, we will have an in-depth discussion on how Europeans developed their will to conquer.

Europeans and Their
Will to Conquer

Why are Europeans motivated by the will to conquer? First, it appears that Europeans were always driven by the will to conquer. They're driven by the extreme conditions of early Stone Age Europe. More accurately, the caveman was a result of the slow-moving pace of the glacial period that occurred sometime during the Wormian Ice Age. The extreme cold temperatures of early Europe forged his European will to live. So, he learned to conquer as a matter of survival.

There is an important phrase coined by Charles Darwin that when spoken is largely misunderstood. "Survival of the fittest" is often misinterpreted to mean "Kill or be killed," a view widely considered by Europeans. The phrase has been the driving force behind their will to conquer. The European has raped, pillaged, and plundered his way throughout world history. In this way, the European will to conquer is, quite possibly, driven by internal mechanisms linked to their genetic makeup.

Now, I am not a geneticist. Nor am I qualified to talk about genetics. I'm not a geographer. But, I offer explanations for changes in both genetics and geography.

Quite simply, Europeans endured two ice ages, the second being the Wormian Ice Age. That's the ice age that turned the Grimaldi's skin white. The Grimaldi's are the earliest ancestors of Europeans. They were Black skinned, curly hair, and typically blue-eyed people who, quite possibly, lived among the Neanderthal. Hence, there was the firm possibility of ad-mixing among the Grimaldi and Neanderthal. Along with close-ordered pair-bonding, those whose phenotype adapted, those whose genetics developed the SLC245 gene adjusted to the extremely cold weather conditions. They survived. While those whose phenotype could not adapt, those whose genetics failed to develop the SLC245 gene simply died out. Sexual selection began to take place. And lighter skinned Grimali-decent Europeans survived.

Fast forward to approximately ten thousand years ago and we began to see modern Europeans for the first time, a people I believe are Cro-Magnon. Due to the treacherous terrains and extreme weather conditions of prehistoric Europe, modern Europeans were nomadic. Many were foragers and survivalists, moving from place-to-place in search of food, water, and shelter. The scarcity of available resources, concubines included, forced early Europeans to conduct tyrant raids on other nomadic tribes in Europe. Raids included the capturing and raping of early Stone Age women and children. They also scavenged in order to survive thus becoming effective at hunting and killing. The one thing they had in common was the extreme conditions that influenced their evolutionary development.

The entire theme of rape, pillage, and plunder was born from the European will to survive. Even the concept of individualism (hence the birth of the rugged individual) derived from the nomadic practices of modern Europeans. Sixty-five thousand years trapped between fire and ice honed their survival skills. Now, their survival instincts became a large part of their genetic makeup. And their genetic makeup controlled much of their personality. In short, the newly evolved racial variation of the original man was battle-hardened. But, was he ready to withstand the test of time?

As the Stone Age passed, modern Europeans made their way beyond Europe and into the rest of the world. From that point, they would rape, pillage, and plunder their way throughout world history, conquering vast empires and civilizations. Due to their tendency to behave in brutish or uncivilized ways, the Persians, who controlled the region at the time of antiquity, were forced to cut off European trade routes.

That's right! Europeans were cut off from the rest of the world once again but, this time by the Persians. Europe deteriorated, falling into economical, intellectual, and cultural decline. The physical separation or isolation from the civilized world caused Europeans to endure a dark age. So, when the Moors set out to civilize Europe, after five hundred years in isolation, they were surprised to see that the European will, forged from the extreme conditions of the European Stone Age, enabled them to survive. The rest of this story picks up when the Moors arrived on the shores of Spain.

The African Presence
in Early Europe

In the beginning of this chapter, we asked the question, "What happened to the Moors?" Well, the relationships of power between the Moors and Spanish shifted, changing the dynamics of their existence. Allow me to explain.

As the story goes, the Moors sailed across the Mediterranean Sea to Europe in an armada of two hundred warships. They appeared off the shores of Spain in 711AD. Their objective was to civilize (Westernize) European nations. During their seven-hundred-year reign in Spain (781 years to be exact), the younger generation of Moors were said to have been a menace to Spanish society. They accosted Spanish women, intimidated the men, and disrespected their children. Thus, the Moors' expulsion from Span was the direct result of their tyranny. Their expulsion was referred to as "a reaction to an internal problem" that affected the already over extended Spanish Empire.

The Spanish were weary or tired from defending the empire against Moorish conquest, hence, a subtle or clever use of expression (weary or tired) to imply fearful. Most were deathly afraid of the Moors. The Vikings, who migrated throughout Europe, became disenchanted with the aggressiveness displayed by the Moors. They returned to their former countries (approx. 1089 AD). There, they enlisted the help of neighboring tribesmen (a Germanic term). They raised an army that would begin to push back the Moors reign in Spain. They even enlisted help from England in an effort to overthrow the Moors. With help from England and neighboring tribesmen, the Vikings would begin to liberate Spain and then Portugal from the imperial rule of their erstwhile allies, marking the beginning of the Crusades or Holy Wars (1095). In all, there were eight major battles fought between Europeans and the Moors. The last Crusades ended 1291AD. Nearly two hundred years later, in 1492, the last Moors were run out of Europe. Since then, Europeans or White people have been conspiring, globally, to oppress Black people.

Symbolic Festivals of Spain

Today, the Moors have no reign in Spain. There is but a two-part celebration symbolic of the European victory over the Moors. It's called Sanfermin or the running of the bulls. The bull symbolizes the fearsome nature of a Moor. The celebration is a summertime festival in preparation of the great bull fights or La Fiesta Brava (the Brave Festival). I'm not going to detail each aspect of the events. That story is best left for another time. But, there is a connection between the two festivals in Spain and the statue of the bull on Wall Street in New York. Called the Charging Bull, or sometimes referred to as the Bull of Wall Street or the Bowling Green Bull, it is believed to be symbolic of slave auctions that were held on Wall Street during the period of US slavery.

Slaves were the original commodity on the New York stock exchange. We do know that slave holders warehoused slaves in dungeons directly underneath Wall Street. Rumor has it, well, what we know to be true in the Black community is that slave holders knew they were auctioning off the Moors as chattel. The famous bronze statue that stands on Broadway north of Bowling Green in the Financial District of Manhattan, New York City is symbolic of the European conquest and victory over the Moors. That's right; for those of you who'd like to know, many of yesterday's Moors, today, refer to themselves as African American. But, let's not get upset about that! It isn't true for every Black American.

Also today, a minority of Black Americans have taken on their ancestors' identity. *Rise of the Moors* is part of the Moorish sovereign movement in which its members believe they are independent citizens of the United Sates thus are not subject to, bound by, nor do they recognize or acknowledge US laws concerning state and federal governments.

Moorish sovereignty adopts an interpretation of a separate law that forms the basis of a political doctrine that recognizes African Americans as an elite class within American society. The doctrine acknowledges that the Moors are endowed with inalienable rights and privileges that grant them sovereign immunity, placing their members beyond state and federal jurisdiction. The identity group, Rise of the Moors, continues to practice Moorish sovereign ideology as the basis of a social, economical, and political program or movement.

The Crusades or Holy Wars

Now, let's back up a bit, not quite to the very end of antiquity, when the Moors first landed in Spain (711AD), but to the beginning of the Crusades (1095). The Crusades were a series of religious wars (some would say) fought between Christians and Muslims. These battles (Holy Wars) were said to start primarily to maintain or seize control of land considered sacred by both groups. Again, there were eight major battles in all during Crusade expeditions, starting from 1095 ending in 1291.

Now, I could detail every aspect of the Holy Wars. But that would be glorifying Christianity in its darkest moments. Besides, these wars were not fought in the name of religion. No, religion was a way for them to validate the bloodshed between immigrants and xenophobes, bloody violence that resulted in mass killings and an inordinate number of injuries accrued over time. You should also know these Holy Wars were raids on entire societies where unsuspecting and innocent citizens were brutally massacred. These so-called crusades were often won by European Christians also making them the dominant force in a fight for sacred land in the Middle East. However, there is another series of stories, often untold, that helped propel Christianity to its current status.

Remember, I said the younger generation of Moors showed a lack of respect for Europeans? Well, the Europeans, greatly disrespected, were mainly from Spain and its people were tired of the Moors bullying Spanish citizens. Both the Moors and Europeans knew war was imminent due to "a [bad] reaction to an internal problem," the problem being a lack of respect for Europeans. Both groups set out across the world to recruit people to fight in the name of religion (1089AD). They appealed to the masses by spreading the gospel (the good news or the word of God) thus beginning the Crusades or Holy Wars.

While the Moors began spreading the word throughout parts of Asia, Christians knew of remote areas in Europe where Europeans lived unaffected by the outside world. Christians formed a relationship with the Vikings early, and perhaps, long before the Moors Westernized Spain (some say 336AD). They were quick to travel along the back coast of Europe to forgotten places of the world. There, Christian monks set out to indoctrinate tribesmen into Christianity. But, it wouldn't be easy.

The Vikings or ancient Teuton people were comfortable practicing Teutonic Mythology. In fact, the Vikings believed in stories as told in Teutonic mythology and Ole Norse tradition, the story of Odin, the main God in Norse mythology. They felt that Christianity lacked in strength and character.

In Viking tradition, during the last day of the year and their coldest day, they sacrificed prisoners of war to appease Odin the Viking God. It is said that the way in which war prisoners were sacrificed would enable the Vikings to communicate with Odin. As the story goes, the Vikings would dismember each prisoner, separating the head, arms, and legs from the torso.

Next, the Vikings hung dismembered body parts from the tallest tree in the forest, the one facing the North Star, said to be where Odin lived. Then, they placed the remaining torsos at the tree roots to be offered as sacred gifts. The bloody body parts soaked the tree roots, said to fill the tree with energy (life) so they could speak directly to Odin.

The Vikings introduced their practice to the Christians who, in turn, took the news back to their religious leaders. Well, news of the Teuton rejection did not sway Christian leaders in the least. After the monks returned, Christian leaders symbolized aspects of Teutonic mythology and then indoctrinated it into the Christian religion.

The monks returned to meet with the Teuton people. This time they introduced Christmas and as a higher form of spiritual worship. They told the Teuton that Christmas was similar to their story about the tree of life. But it was more powerful than the literal translation of the ole Norse tradition and Teutonic worship. The Teuton people eventually accepted Christianity, becoming the last European tribe to adopt Christian religion. The adorning of the tree during Christmas celebration became a new practice in Christianity.

The tree of life, as it was called is, today, symbolized by Christians as the Christmas tree. It is used in celebration and symbolic representation of the birth of Jesus Christ (Jesus of Nazareth). But, there are many ornaments on the Christmas tree that symbolizes Teutonic worship.

The traditional red balls on a Christmas tree symbolize the dismembered heads placed on the tree limbs that the Teuton people used to adorn their sacred tree. The arms and legs are represented by candy canes, which sit on the limbs of today's Christmas trees. The red and white stripes on a candy cane symbolize the blood running down the lifeless remains of war prisoners. And the blood-soaked roots of the tree are denoted by a red cloth found wrapped around the base of the Christmas tree.

Next is the star that sits atop the tree. It is generally recognized as the Star of Bethlehem (also the Jewish symbol of King David or the Star of David), which is associated with the Christian cross or martyrdom. It is also viewed as the Northern most star, which guided the three Kings of Orient on their journey to Bethlehem. More importantly, it symbolizes the home of Odin, the ole Viking God. As for the presents placed at the tree base during Christmas holidays, it is supposed to represent the many gifts given to baby Jesus, the new born king. As a matter of fact, what it symbolizes is the gruesome torsos placed at the bottom of the tree during Teutonic worship, offerings to the Viking God for greater success in future battles.

Last is Christian hand symbols used for prayer. Christians are taught to use hand symbols to pray. They often pray with their hands folded or shaped in the form of a pyramid. The pyramid often symbolizes the ability to communicate with a higher power. Well, fact of the matter is Christian hand symbols represent the tree of life (the nine realms of Asgard protected by Odin) and the ability to communicate with the Viking God Odin. End of story.

While the story of the Christmas tree is accurate, the story, name, date of birth, and location of Jesus are not. The story behind the birth of Christ, called an immaculate conception, was taken from the ancient Egyptian funerary text, Book of the Dead. In the Book of the Dead, it gives an account of Isis and the birth of her son Horus as the oldest documented version of the Immaculate Conception. Some scholars claim it happened on December 25th while others believe it occurred January 6th or 7th. The latter dates coincide with Teutonic worship.

The story of the Immaculate Conception was adopted by the Romans in the year 325-6AD. It was approved by General Constantine. Constantine the Great (306 – 337) was the first Roman emperor to convert to Christianity. At the first annual meeting for the council of Nicaea (nai·see·uh, 325AD), the decision was made to convert the citizens of Rome to Christianity. They change the names of Roman deities, giving them Christian names. Names like Saint Mark, Luke, and Mathews are European names they gave in order to perpetuate a legacy of White superiority. As for the birth name of Christ, the name "Jesus" came much later.

It wasn't until the fifteenth (some say sixtieth) century that the letter "J" was added to the English alphabet. Before then, it was not a part of old English vocabulary. Nor was it a part of Hebrew (Aramaic) language. Even to this day, the letter "J" is not a part of Hebrew language. The rightful name of Christ, lord our savor, is Ye'shua (meaning to rescue). The name Jesus is a fictitious biblical character invented to sell White supremacy. However, there were several people who earned to title Christ. But, we will not discuss them today.

It was Pope Alexander, VI, who used his son as a symbol of worship and image of Christ. As the story goes, Pope Alexander was tired of his people praying to a Black savior (Ye'shua). Pope Julius II headed the Roman Catholic Church and ruled the Papal States (1503 – 1513). He commissioned Michelangelo to create a Europeanized version of Christ. Had Michelangelo refused, the Pope promised to behead him and have his remains brought to his chambers on a silver platter. Michelangelo, who had no conception of a White Christ, used his homosexual lover as the model for the imagery. He painted a mural of Christ on the ceiling of the Sistine Chapel.

As a special note of importance, the story about the birth of Christ is a fictitious account assumed to be true for religious purposes regardless of whether it is or not. The truth is Christ all mighty never resided in Israel. In fact, his Ethiopian mother, who's identified by the European name Mary, never made the trip to Israel. Ye'shua was born and raised in Ethiopia. He later died in the mountains of Ethiopia as told by the first Christians.

During the Renaissance Era, the Roman Catholic Church was extremely dangerous. It was responsible for the most brutal, violent and often heinous, crimes committed in the name of Christianity. The rape, pillage, and plundering of countless civilizations were often committed under the rule of the Roman Catholic Church. The Catholic Church used liberty, religion, and other fraudulent means to justify violence against innocent people, committing mass murders in the name of religion, often causing severe damage to entire nations and vast civilizations.

In this chapter, we found the reason behind the European will to conquer. In the process, we also uncovered certain myths and misconceptions about Christian religion. In the next chapter, we will discuss more on the European will to conquer by exploring The Context of European Aggression. The question of whether or not Europeans will ever unlearn their source of aggression, racism and sexism, lies ahead.

Chapter 2
The Context of European Aggression

Who included me among the ranks of the human race?

Joseph Brodsky (1940 – 1996)

Scholars have always speculated about living in extreme temperatures. Some say extreme weather conditions could preserve physical aspects of one's identity. For example, the White race is thought to be free of genetic impurities from not reproducing with races that fail to share heritable characteristics. This belief is, in part, due to the climate endured by Whites during the Ice Age. People like Joseph Brodsky are proud of their racial heritage. They have no problem identifying as a separate and distinct race from nonwhites. They also credit their preservation and intelligence to the Ice Age. Still more scholars, the Afrocentrists, say, while the Ice Age may have forged the European will to conquer, it caused irreparable damage to their race as a whole. The result is their behavior causes problems that have severe consequences for the entire world.

As we consider the content found in this book, we recognize the importance of discussing race. We are returning to an old worldview that humans are made up of separate and distinct races. Over the centuries, this view has been the leading problem source behind White aggression, racism and sexism. Yet, it continues to exist at the center of controversy to this day.

One of my main goals in this chapter and throughout the entirety of this book is to form a link between race and evolution. Both our identity and early development are related to environmental experiences and situational influences that shape our perception of the world and how others perceive us in it. It's how we cope with those perceptions that give us purposeful meaning. Since people have become perceptually ignorant to the concept of race—perhaps in hoping it would go away—you need to understand it better and learn how to use it in ways that are more productive.

The Evolution of Human Races

Years ago, scholars were inclined to believe that humans evolved from the same species, just not the same race. Well, I'm old school. I don't believe in throwing out the baby with the bath water. I believe we should exhaust all of our avenues until we arrive at a proper conclusion as I have come to form my own conclusions.

Although we originally came from one race, the human race, it is no longer true of humans. Regardless of their ill-intentions, Europeans are right when they say we belong to different races. In fact, we have evolved into different races. However, we still belong to the same species: Human beings.

The term race implies there are very few characteristic differences among people. It also implies there is little variation in the adaptive behavioral traits we share, much like the Neanderthal. In fact, for the Neanderthal and, perhaps, earlier primates, there was very little variation among them.

Since the Neanderthal were nomadic and lived in small groups, they were codependent on one another to survive. They existed like interrelated parts that functioned, collectively, each one having their own unique skill the others needed to survive, perhaps struggling to exist as a community. Therefore, they were cognitively undeveloped. They also mimicked primates who came into contact with them as part of their dependency. The lack of variation in adaptive behavior is, perhaps, the very reason why they died out. Besides, the notion of one big happy race ignores important aspects of natural selection.

So, we're still one big happy race, are we? Well, let's see! It's quite possible that at one point in time our prehistoric ancestors were one big race, mimicking behavior to adapt or learn. But, thanks to natural selection, today, we do not operate as our prehistoric ancestors. The way we think, what we say, and everything we do is influenced by where we come from, the people with whom we interact, and the things that happen to us. In fact, our behavior occurs in cultural context. (The context or social settings in which we live may very well be the reason why we do not live as prehistoric or Stone Age man did. I am well aware of that.) Homes, schools, churches, cities, states, and countries, even barren land with miles of rugged terrain form the environment within which we live. Regardless of where we are in the world, we adapt our behavior to the environment and grow in intellect. The Neanderthal did not grow in intellect until they ad-mixed with the Grimaldis or, perhaps, the Cro-Magnon who are responsible for the Neanderthal going extinct.

According to the world-famous Naturalist, Charles Darwin, natural selection is the process by which species better adapted to survive in their environment achieve greater reproductive success. Each species, in turn, pass genetic advantages onto future generations. The genetic advantage ensures their survivability. It also means certain genes will die out with each evolutionary cycle.

The upside of natural selection is the process by which each member, born to later generations, will possess favorable traits. This is exactly why we, as humans, share similar characteristic temperaments and associated behavior. But, no two humans are exactly alike. We differ immensely in our physical characteristics. But, there are only so many personality types humans inherit as a whole. In fact, people differ enough that scientists spend the better part of their existence trying to prove how uniquely different we are from one another. And rightly so! Europeans were isolated from the outside world for tens of millennia. Truly, there has to be some difference that exists between us.

What scientists learned from the European experience was cultural factors like historical, economical, social, and others contribute to differences in human perception, making them uniquely different. The difference is not vast. But, it makes us one of a kind. We know about genetic differences too. Yet, we still know nothing about the genes for skin color. In fact, most of our differences are superficial. Hair texture, size and shape of head, shape of our nose and face, et cetera. Truth of the matter is the way we perceive the world makes us uniquely different. But, collectively, we're not all that different. Our origins are the same: African!

We often endure certain environmental experiences and situational influences that shape who we are to become. Or, these experiences and influences mold our perception of the world. It's the way we endure that makes us distinctive, especially any qualities that set the tone for the way we behave, think, and feel. For example, we generally have the same level of tolerance for behavior. What we endure can have a powerful or dramatic impact on us. Where we differ is in the coping mechanisms needed to successfully deal with difficult problems or our current situation.

As we continue to evolve, scholars need to address humanity in contexts, such as global interdependence, which helps determine the nature of relationships and the power that continuously shifts between people. As you increase your cultural awareness in life, you may become more sensitive to the problem of race. You may even live to see evolution create dynamic changes in role reversal. You may also become more attuned to how context shapes your own beliefs and behaviors.

Whites and Blacks in Contrast

Blacks are in a uniquely different situation than Whites. Blacks have been subjected to cruel forms of domination. Most are born into it. Others, and I mean a unique few, are surrounded by it. Either way, the impact has an immediate and strong effect on Black people. In contrast, the White experience is quite the opposite. Whites are socially dominant, which means they are largely in control.

Their beliefs or assumptions about nonwhites make it hard for them to have continuous, first-hand contact with Blacks, strangers, and others. Their condescending attitudes are tell-tale signs that Whites want no interactions with them. Many Whites believe they have the ability to surpass Blacks in intellect and achievements. And rightly so! For five hundred years, they have asserted their dominance over Blacks, nonwhites, and strangers. Slavery, eugenics, and now the reemergence of old-fashioned racism and White supremacy tell the world that Whites can dominate at will. Truly, one could say Whites are the superior race.

If aggression is a key component to achieving superiority, then Whites are truly superior. Their level of aggression makes them appear uniquely superior. Historically, Whites displayed aggression to show dominance. They also exploited their intelligence to show superiority. Some would say they appear to have an abundance of both. The problem is they would not have been able to exploit their intelligence had they failed to oppress Blacks, for example. Also, the words dominance and superiority are being used interchangeably. Clearly, dominance is connected to aggression, which is not a measure of superiority. As well, superiority in the context of race does not define dominance. Here, well-defined definitions would be beneficial, right?

You can look up both definitions and contrast each one with aggression. But, I will supply some for you.

Dominance or *social dominance* is nothing more than having the ability to exert power over others. *Intelligence* is the ability to profit from experience. But all you need to know is that no one race is more intelligent than another. Each race has equally intelligent and unintelligent members. No matter where you are in the world, or in the universe for that matter, you will find equally intelligent and unintelligent beings. Therefore, intelligence is universal. Aggression, on the other hand, is not.

There are social forces that factor into aggression. For example, the extreme conditions of early Europe made it nearly possible for prehistoric Europeans to survive. Those who survive developed an aggressive nature from enduring its cruel and harsh conditions. Here, we need an operational definition for racial aggression. Why? It's not wise to accept assumptions about human nature at face value however plausible it sounds.

Racial aggression is any hostile attitude or behavior, especially a hostile action directed against other races or racial groups, often without provocation. You should also know the definition for species, race, ethnicity, culture, and nationality in order to follow along in our discussion. Later, and throughout the remainder of this book, it would serve to remember these definitions.

Species are any group of organisms that can mate and produce offspring also having the ability to reproduce. *Race* is defined as any group of organisms divided on the basis of phenotype. Hair texture, the shape of nose and face, skin color, and other physical traits help determines one's race. *Ethnicity* is defined by shared beliefs and values found in a group. Members from the same church or people who follow the same social customs and belief systems, regardless of racial orientation, define one's ethnicity. *Culture* is defined by the social customs and traditions that help establish our institutions. In other words, you can usually tell which culture a person is from simply by the customs and traditions they follow. And, *nationality* is identified by one's national status or citizenship. People often use these terms interchangeably with race. But, it's often race we think of whenever we use such terms.

Even today, people substitute the word race for ethnicity under the assumption that one word has a better definition. Neither word does! Race has nothing to do with ethnicity and vice versa. Also, at one point in history, Whites defined race by nationality. The Irish was considered a different race than the English. The French considered themselves to be completely different from the Germans, et cetera. Unfortunately, when speaking of race, they were referring to nationality or, better, their national identity.

Different languages also helped to create social distance among the many European nations. People like Alexander Pushkin, a West African Moor and the father of Russian language, created greater distinction among Russia and the many European nations. From that point onward, Russians believed they had evolved into a separate and distinct race. Remember, ethnicity is what most people mean when they think about the concept of race. Again, we can see that one word has nothing to do with the other.

During the fifteenth and sixteenth century, and perhaps the latter half of the fourteenth century, there was a push to define race by intelligence. By that time, the Catholic Church was undergoing tremendous change. A new form of slavery was emerging. Europeans were responsible for the destruction of Black civilizations. In fact, Blacks suffered several loses starting with the battle of Carthage in the second Punic War, the fall of Jerusalem, the loss of Kemet, and other great African civilizations like the Kingdom of Kush. King Ferdinand, II, and Queen Isabella, I, of Castile issued an edict stating that any person or persons declared savage (cannibals) could be enslaved, indefinitely.

The Catholic Church spitefully labeled Africans savage (e.g., Hannibal the cannibal) in order to justify their enslavement. Pope Innocent, VIII, received a gift of one hundred Africans as chattel, which gave rise to the idea of using Blacks, perpetually, as slaves. He, in turn, granted Portugal the right to enslave Africans below the Saharan, indefinitely. Now, Africans in the civilized world were considered to exist beneath the collar of Whites. Then up sprang the idea of proposed religious improvement backed, granted, or fully indorsed by the sanctity of the church. All of the efforts made were to separate White Europeans from nonwhites for proposed human improvement.

The idea of selective breeding was proposed by Sir Francis Galton, the father of eugenics, and cousin to the famous Naturalist Charles Darwin. Although the concept had no name at the time, European scientists would propose the improvement of humans by encouraging reproduction only with those having heritable characteristics regarded as desirable. Eugenics grew increasingly popular with researchers in the scientific community. That is to say, until it was discredited as unscientific and its doctrines viewed as racist during the late twentieth century. Unfortunately, many countries continue to engage in the practice, the United States practicing, secretly, well into the new millennium. It was the eugenics movement that perpetuated the belief that Europeans are superior to nonwhites.

Europeans made a concerted effort to propose their superiority. They conquered a great part of the civilized world. Western technology is an expression of that aggression. Science and technology advanced as a result of European conquest. The development of machines, equipment, and systems had a dramatic and far-reaching effect on the European will. Starting with the relationships of power shifting from Blacks to Whites, the Europeanized doctrine of Christian religion, the institution of slavery, and two eugenics movements, Europeans used racial aggression as a method to conquer and siege control of the Black race. As you can tell, European aggression is the primary reason why the world conforms to Western expectations. Today, weapons, science, and computer technology are created, not only to give an advantage to Europeans but, to ensure their dominance in the world.

Unwitting Participants

Black inventors add to the growth of America's intellectual potential. They create some of the most extraordinary inventions on earth. However, Europeans continue take full credit for most of their inventions and breakthroughs, even well into the twenty-first century. They claim the most important discoveries, especially in science, medicine, and technology. Hell, if it were up to Europeans, they'd claim to be the original people. Oh, that's right, they already made that claim. But, I digress.

The problem is a host of important inventions are created by Blacks. Their inventions, discoveries, and major breakthroughs are pivotal in America, becoming, perhaps, the leading innovators of technology in global history. Some short-sighted Blacks inventors like Garrett Morgan, Granville T. Woods, and Patricia Era Bath made major contributions to America, contributions that would forward European progress or advance the White man's cause.

Black inventors became unwitting participates of Western imperialism. Many Black inventions were created to save lives. Garrett Morgan invented the gas mask, which he demonstrated, live, when coal miners were trapped by poisonous gas in a mining accident. The mask was so effective that the government quickly deployed its use in World War I. The gas mask protected soldiers from the poisonous effects of chloride gas, becoming America's greatest defense against nuclear, biological, and chemical warfare.

Then there are those nonwhites who ignorantly contribute to European progress or Western imperialism. These are the people who seek out positive relations with the larger, dominant culture. They're often told that their production contributes to the betterment of American society as a whole. So, they relinquish their cultural identity and move into the larger society. In this way, they believe they can become more productive. There, in the larger society, they adapt new lifestyles that come from having continuous, first-hand contact with Whites.

Many of these nonwhites become affluent or come from affluent backgrounds. They seek employment in career fields such as researcher, scientist, architect, engineer, et cetera, anywhere where they can be of service to America. Often, they are unaware that their skills and talents are being adapted for use as weapons of mass destruction. Others, who try to fit in where they can, are well aware of their actions. There is an entirely different process to understanding their psyche. They often want nothing more to do with their own people. They place their values before those of others. Their concern is with self-preservation or preserving their own individual interests. So, they have a close rank mentality and will disregard members of their own race to protect their self-interest. They're often called gatekeepers.

Gatekeepers will often take it upon themselves to decide who should have rights or access to public accommodations. Public accommodations include having access to spaces like fair-housing, better communities, restaurants, et cetera. Gatekeepers also prevent nonwhites from establishing hereditary entitlements that control access to official positions of power.

I'm not going to have an in-depth discussion on politics here. Why not? This book is not about that! But, I will leave you with enough information to give you insight on how complex a situation gatekeeping can be. Now, if we were to consider politics, especially the conservative aspects of Republicanism, you will come to learn that many nonwhites have a close rank mentality. As gatekeepers, they believe it is their inherent right to control, block, or defer access to other nonwhites who are ready to assume official positions of authority that wield political power.

First, there are many reasons why a person might gatekeep. And, every reason why is validated in his or her own mind. The wrong age, for example, or being too disabled, feared as being receptive to violence, and race, color, and sexual orientation are all valid concerns for a gatekeeper when considering the perceived dangers of working with nonwhites.

For whatever reasons, gatekeeping has higher priority in certain situations. In a workplace setting, for example, where minority hiring is mandatory, it is more useful to have an Afro-Latino/a employed. That way, you hire a double minority who often shares your views about the minority half of their dual heritage.

Gatekeepers can be found most anyplace, that is to say, the workplace, church, or politics. Wherever their social status can be compromised, you will find gatekeepers protecting, promoting, or forwarding the White man's cause. In this example, it was White male politicians who were gatekeeping. They limited women access to the US President during the Obama administration. Their intentions were to prevent women from receiving promotions ahead of White males in the administration.

Curiously, many of the women who wanted access to President Obama were nonwhite.

Obama took quick action to assure women had equal access to him and his senior staff. He also elected Susan Elizabeth Rice as the US Ambassador for the United Nations from 2009 to 2013. But, it didn't stop there. President Obama appointed Susan Rice as the twenty-fourth US National Security Advisor from 2013 to 2017. And in one of his many deeds, President Obama signed new executive orders to enforce equal pay for women.

The problem was many of the women who benefited under his administration became extensions of power or authority under Western imperialism. What made their situation problematic was Obama believed in empire-building. President Obama was issued an international mandate. He was to take on the task of acquiring greater power and authority by extending America's influence over countries like Libya. But, it was Susan Rice who ended up taking the fall.

Susan Elizabeth Rice took the fall for an attack on Benghazi, Libya, an attack that destroyed several CIA facilities and left four CIA employees dead. The attack on Susan Rice was made to tarnish her image and, hopefully, have her removed from a position of power. This was a problem of racism and sexism in the workplace environment. In this case, conservative politicians attempted to gatekeep or close ranks on a double minority to ensure her servility. Their goal was to ensure that the ambassadorship would forever remain a position for men, White men.

Gatekeepers are largely found anywhere where there is opportunity to advance. You have to remember that gatekeeping is an agreement used, in part, as a quid pro quo deal. Even when a deal has not been made, a favor or an advantage is expected in return for keeping the tradition of White male supremacy alive.

After years of gatekeeping, for example, Michael Steele was appointed the first Black chairman of the GOP (Grand Old Party), an appointment he never thought he'd receive. Steele had been passed over so many times and for various positions in office that when he was appointed head of the GOP, he quickly overwhelmed himself, sub-consciously thwarting his own objectives.

Nonwhites who tend to gatekeep may get some consolation in knowing that other nonwhites will not have a chance to earn their place among some potential racial hierarchy. For the gatekeeper, it does not matter if a member of his or her own race is discriminated against. Every effort made to gatekeep or close ranks brings them closer to securing access to official positions of power.

However, you must also remember, gatekeeping is wrong under most circumstances. An exception to this rule might be cultural appropriation. Why? Whenever you choose to appropriate someone else's culture, it is perceived to be an extension of power or authority over a people in the interests of domination: otherwise known as cultural imperialism.

The power of Western influence is staggering. The unwitting participation of nonwhites tell us how far people will go to find social acceptance or to become part of the

European will, even if it means being cruel or brutal toward their own. Why? For some people, the idea of belonging satisfies their personal needs, rewards them, raises self-esteem, gives them identity, and a sense of purpose or meaning. For others, they find solace in belonging to a higher power. Still, nonwhites have a need to do what is necessary to survive a dangerous situation. Basically, belonging rewards people either materially or psychologically.

In the next chapter, we will look at the motivation behind Western technology. There, we will have a chance to look deeper into the context of European aggression.

Chapter 3
The Motivation Behind Western Technology

It is appalling to learn that Western technology is an expression of White aggression.

Brian C. McGuire, In Press

Western technology is motivated by aggression. It's not just open-ended aggression, either. It is greatly driven by racial conflict and hatred. More than any application of science used in conquest, Western technology is well-known for its collaboration of systems and techniques used to create weapons of mass destruction.

Albert Einstein once said, "It has become appallingly obvious that our technology has exceeded our humanity." Einstein, though not a deeply opinionated fellow, had strong convictions about the direction in which the world was headed. He knew that holding at their present course, Whites would commit an act far worse than global destruction. What Einstein knew was that Western technology would make Whites lose their sense of humanity, a questionable quality that has always been at-risk among Whites.

Technology plays an important role in how we perceive the world today. The application of guns in America bears on this discussion. On December 1, 2021, four grade school students were killed while seven others were injured during a mass shooting at Oxford High School in Oxford, Michigan. The lone gunman, himself a student at Oxford High, offered authorities no motive for the shootings. What was the moral reasoning behind Ethan Crumbley's display of deadly force?

In 2016, the Los Angeles Cubs won the World Series against the Cleveland Indians. Fans supporting both teams set multiple fires to the downtown area of Cleveland, apparently, in shock at the long overdue victory, others over the great upset. Fires turned into rioting and looting. A night of bedlam, it was pure and utter chaos on the streets of Cleveland, Ohio. No police were called in to contain the groups of rowdies causing problems on the streets.

Since the Trump administration, violence against Blacks has increased considerably. State-sanctioned violence, even murder against Black people by White police officers when situations do not call for such violence, shows that America is less accepting toward Blacks than in the past 2 decades. An angry crowd of Blacks form a protest against systemic abuse and police violence. The government response is to dispatch an armored personnel unit to restore order even before clarifying the situation or publicly announcing the circumstances surrounding it.

America is obviously growing out of control. For Whites, it's the cultural attitude that the vast majority of nonwhites are unintelligent and driven by the violent aspects of life, which means Whites must protect themselves at all cost. But, in actuality, Whites are giving lip service. Underneath, they harbor profoundly racist feelings.

Whites have a very aggressive nature thus are preoccupied with physical rather than emotional or spiritual needs. It is the sum of their practical knowledge with regard to the material culture that I speak of today. Much like Abraham Maslow and his hierarchy of human motives, Whites are preoccupied with basic material needs, which impede their full potential of becoming creative, talented, and healthy-minded people.

Whites say that the world fails to see their tenacity for preserving their genetic heritage, which allows every member to possess favorable traits. The idea is for them to evolve separately so that they can consider the forward thrust of life. Such preservation enables them to push into the hostilities of the current environment so they can fulfill their potential of becoming fully functioning people. In stark contrast, most of them push to create a hostile environment to hold their grounds in an effort to adapt, develop, and evolve as they so choose, not what nature intended them to become. In this way, they firmly believe humans are in control of their own destiny.

Most White people believe that racial diversity equals genocide. Many of them believe that the entire idea of integration upsets the natural circle of life. That if they were to integrate with nonwhites, for example, the White race would simply die out. In this way, they feel as if they are in a fight to preserve their genetic heritage. Today, they try to preserve it. They try to prevent the current quality or condition of their lives from any changes that would lead to degeneration or, simply, losing a legacy of gains, an advantage or improvement they acquired over time.

Whites are anxious to preserve their genetic heritage. They live with the understanding that their genetic material favors reproduction by some people more than others. So, they seek to preserve their genetic heritage from harm, especially harm against people whose biology is considered undesirable.

Artificial selection favors selective breeding as proposed improvement of human society. The idea or intended goal is for people, specifically White people, to become better or complex beings. They fear that cannot happen when humans develop as a result of undesirable changes in heritable characteristics. So, they propose improvement of their race by encouraging the reproduction of genetic characteristics considered desirable.

Recent developments in in vitro fertilization or family balancing, advancements for accelerating incubation in the field of science, and the latest laser technology as a way to cure cancer, each serves to preserve the integrity of life and to advance the reproduction of people who are considered desirable. For Whites, the benefit of developing Western medical technology is to gain that advantage over the rest of human society. The evolution of democracy in Europe and North America diminishes that very idea. Artificial selection (the practice of Eugenics) is one way to diminish democracy in the Western world.

North Americans have been leading the advancement of technology for the past 200 hundred plus years. Starting, perhaps, with the economic development of rural-agriculture and urban-industrialization, Whites had a critical hand in developing modern Western civilization. They were also responsible for the way Western modes of behavior and production influence all parts of the world. The production of automobiles, air planes, locomotion or steam trains, advancement of the traffic light, and many more Western inventions actually influenced the course of cultural evolution.

Contrary to popular belief, it is possible to make distinctions between Western technology and features of nonwestern technology. Phones, automobiles, and computerized technological innovations are products of Western civilization. Each one adds or changes the general advancement of Western society and its industry greatly, especially given the considerable influence practical knowledge has over the material culture.

It's the sum of a society's practical knowledge that adds value to or changes to its material culture. It can determine which direction a society is headed as a matter of progress. The Western world has made considerable progress with regard to physical wellness opposed to emotional or spiritual wellness. The Eastern world continues to make innovative progress with regard to emotional or spiritual wellness. Both forms of progression are hallmarks in terms of technological innovation. Today, it's the Western world that stands on the cutting edge of technology. Like in a well-known television series The Six Million Dollar Man, the West has the technology to make you better, stronger, and faster than any other person on earth. And that's because there's been a push to surpass other nations in intellect, achievement, and ability.

The push for technology has given Whites added advantage. Although, their advantage has not come without great cost and suffering. For example, advances in industrialism and technology brought the world pollution, toxic waste, and a host of medical problems, such as cancer. As a way to correct these problems, Whites turned to animal research. But how ethical is research with animals anyway?

There's been massive advancement in research and technology. For generations, researchers conducted research on animals to gain a better understanding of, and to find solutions for, many problems people have today:

- Medication for psychotherapy and behavioral therapy
- Training or therapy for neuromuscular disorders
- Discovery and testing in the treatment of drugs to reduce or alleviate anxiety and severe mental health disorders
- Education or information on alleviating the effects of stress, pain, and related discomfort
- Education or information on drug addiction and relapse
- Application of medical care to help premature infants gain the weight needed to leave the hospital sooner
- Education or information used to reduce or alleviate memory loss for premature senility middle or old age due to generalized degeneration of the brain, et cetera

The problem is such innovations or discoveries result from correcting previous problems with technology. For example, toxic waste is often used or contaminated water from domestic, industrial, or mining applications. The contaminant produces chemical or waste products, which pollutes the air, soil, and sometimes drinking water. The result is the development of about 17 new forms of cancer and genetic diseases like neuromuscular disorders.

Since toxins create a host of diseases, scientists are forced to break into separate and distinct groups to correct medical problems caused by Western technology. Animal research and testing spare researchers the discomfort of experimenting on humans. It does not stop animal killings in the name of research, however. Nor is it a way to reduce the abuse in animal research testing. It is a way to reduce or substitute the pain and suffering humans would endure during clinical trials. However, it's hardly progress when Western civilization substitutes human experimentation for research testing on animals. But, how ethical are people who use animal research to counteract human problems that results from mistakes in advancing technology?

A Wolf in Sheep's Clothing

Beware of any people who disguise their ruthless nature through science and technological innovation. Their scientific curiosity may be subtle signs of aggression. Aggression has taken Western technology to the forefront of discovery. The United Sates has been identified by the world's leading scientists as having an exceptional talent for creating and advancing technology. New innovations, discoveries, improved production, increasing materialism, and advanced technology shows how ready Whites are to lead in the new millennium. And with Western technology leading the way, Whites are free to continue their push for westward expansion and globalization.

Curiously, most technological breakthroughs in the West are the results of amassing important resources. The arrogance comes into play when Whites show contempt for countries that become a part of Western expansion. European progress or White aggression is the motivation behind it all.

Technology helps the Western world progress at a rapid rate. It continues to be the driving force behind Western progression. No one society has progressed at the level that America has with the exception of countries swayed or influenced largely by Western progression. As a matter of fact, Americans know the United States is quite possibly the most productive country on earth. And that fuels their arrogance.

Much like the indigenous people they encountered while acquiring land over the centuries, Whites feel like the remaining world is pagan. So once they acquire land and its natural resources, Whites no longer find local inhabitants useful. This causes White people to take advantage of various races around the world. Their material culture readily reflects that level of arrogance.

Many countries are westernized today. Japan is greatly westernized. Even China is becoming progressive although it's miles to go with the communist country. The Western world is influencing every corner of the globe. And that's a considerable problem.

The problem is the world has begun to socially conform to Western expectations. Conformity places countries like the United States in a position of power. In places like Japan and other parts of the Eastern world, the cultural mainstream is extremely westernized. Fancy cars, luxury homes, some greatly influenced by Western architecture, and trophy spouses tell the world that Eastern nations are adopting the customs, practices, and beliefs of people from Europe and North and South America. And with the Eastern world adopting the corrupt morals of Western society, symbolizing the injustices of racism, the remaining world must now come to terms with itself. People from every walk of life must now consider life by looking through an entirely new lens or be forced to view it through the aesthetic lens of White male supremacy.

Many developing countries are not even invited to join in the advancements of technology in the new millennium. Many times, they lack in important resources. Others offer considerable manpower. These countries seek out new opportunities to advance, especially advancement that combines favorable circumstances or situations. The Western world uses small developing countries in specific ways, which allows them to achieve personal gains, usually by way of exploitation.

Their mistakes work to the advantage of Whites. The Western world takes advantage of developing countries as a customary practice. Land, minerals, and other precious resources are more often targeted by Western countries promising to liberate developing countries. Often due to compromise, government officials believe they are making vast mistakes. Most times, their mistake is in following suit. Others give in or tend to give in to the demands and authority of Western governments. Interestingly, the West has the advantage of technology working at its discretion. Many developing countries do not. It's the endless possibilities that convince developing countries to become part of the technological age.

The ability of technology to change a society's general state or mode of existence, especially one characterized by poverty or suffering, is crucial in determining which society will lead the world in innovation and reach a state of greater civilization. The idea of a developing country being invited to change its situation has exchangeable value. But, as proven, change comes with consequences.

Considerable Consequences
for Change

Loss of tradition or heritage, social customs or cultural practices, and failing belief systems create unstable circumstances that have consequences for mental and physical health. A country could also see an increase in family abuse, substance abuse, homicide, and suicide. Further, it could see conflict and tension come to a point where a resolution is needed.

Other crises may occur, indicating that the country has members who are unsupportive of change. They may choose to resist while other members of the country choose to relinquish their cultural identity and assimilate. The

Western world is always putting pressure on developing countries to conform. Such pressure results in the West expanding its territories. It also pushes for the rest of the world to globalize its resources. Globalizing is especially important for social institutions, such as banks, hospitals, and educational institutions. Why? The quicker developing countries conform to Western expectations, the sooner Western countries can assimilate and gain from foreign resources.

Western countries have little to no respect for the morals and customs of indigenous people in developing countries. Government officials tend to be dishonest with community, cultural, and ethnic groups about their agendas, especially when their plans violate local sensibilities. Depending on the advancement of a country, westerners impose their beliefs and try to change situations that, most times, they were not invited to change.

Westerners often teach countries to impose some-thing compulsory, such as tax or a punishment, on its people. They impose change on smaller, less developed countries in order to assimilate them so that differences are minimized or eliminated or sometimes to target natural resources that are, perhaps, not up for bargaining. In other developing countries, assimilation is part of an agreement reached between two governments in which each promise to fulfill important obligations.

For example, a commercial agreement reached between two countries to fix and preserve natural reserves so business can resume. Petroleum, oil, and natural gas reserves, these resources are naturally occurring raw materials that can be exploited to gain benefits. Unfortunately, Western countries take unfair advantage of the situation and people, usually for personal gain. For example, after the United States liberated Iraq from the dictator Saddam Hussein, the military stole billions of dollars in Iraqi oil from its natural oil reserves. Today, the Iraqi government has yet to recover payment for its lost or stolen resources.

Western technology is said to come as a blessing in disguise. It is said to have the ability to bring an end to world problems. For example, Western technology can end the problem of illness, disorder, and injury to the world by medical treatment. The problem is its depleting the world of its natural resources. And we can't stop feeding this problem child. Western technology has depleted much of the world's resources. And, there are only two regions on the planet that can accommodate this mainstream problem child.

The Middle East and Africa are perhaps the last two areas on the planet that can fuel this technological juggernaut. The problem is many countries in Africa are afraid to conduct business with Western powers like the United States. As for the Middle East, it's been conducting business with Whites for quite some time. They've learned from past mistakes how to conduct business with Western powers. The food for oil program was a valuable lesson for them to learn.

The United Nations sanctioned Iraq in the past for disobeying international laws. As a result, Iraq was cut off from trade routes in which the Iraqi people were not able to attain important resources necessary for their survival. Western governments seized the opportunity and forced Iraq to participate in what the United States called the food for oil program. They were forced to give Western countries oil in exchange for food, clothing, and other important necessities. Since then, they've learned how to negotiate important matters with all nations in exchange for gain or benefits.

Many nations in Africa choose to not conduct business with Western nations. They learned from America's notorious representation that once the West gets a firm footing in Africa, its people are going to steal natural resources, usually by force of arms. As an alternative approach to conducting business with Western powers, African nations are turning to communist countries. Places like Kenya want these countries to support and defend its people and all possessions to include its natural resources from the tyranny of Western imperialism.

There is organic matter from outer space found in South Africa's Micon Draw Mountains. How did that happen? Meteorites crashed into South Africa millions of years ago and formed the Micon Draw Mountains. Much like in the movie Black Panther, these mountains have barely been mined for its resources. Entire mountains are said to be made up of precious metals so rare that it can only be found in South Africa. That makes South Africa a prime target for Western exploitation. Many areas in Africa have yet to be exploited for its potential to produce important resources. Sadly, tremendous efforts to conquer, be it people, land, or important resources, is getting out of control. And with technology's rapid growth potential, the Western world will consume the planet, depleting it of its precious resources in the years to come.

Most of the failures to advance Western technology reflect an unruly or unmanageable people who are out of control. Much of the progress made in the world is fueled by Western arrogance. For example, much of the world believes that global warming will continue unless the United States takes action to bring the problem to an end. This form of thinking is woven into the dependent idea that the United States is superior to other countries. We had plenty of We Are the World moments involving major crises to include world hunger, gang violence, thermo nuclear global warming, two world wars, bordering on the brink of a third world war, often getting into more complex or advance problems, most of which the general public will never know about. However, the progress made to resolve the world's crises was and is often caused by the arrogance of Whites in Northern and Western parts of the world.

Western technology is the result of White people's arrogance. Whites assume that the world wants them to lead humanity in the new millennium. Whites are satisfied in knowing that in many parts of the world, countries are dependent on them for important resources and to modernize their societies. So a lot of the faulty or unstable technology goes to these countries as a result. There, Whites can develop stable prototypes by experimentation. Anyone reluctant to experiment within Western society can conduct important test cases in developing countries without the repercussions of consequences. Arrogantly, part of their hidden agenda is to exploit people and local resources by way of experimentation.

Now, that's not to say Whites haven't experimented on their own people in Western parts of the world. The United States, for example, is notoriously known for experimenting on its private citizens. For example, the eugenics movement was a segregation and sterilization process. Many people who were thought to have undesirable hereditary characteristics were made infertile. Others, who were thought to be incompetent, were permanently housed in mental health facilities across America. Both were susceptible to harm as mental health facilities conducted experimental testing on Whites and Blacks alike. Lobotomies, electroshock therapy, and behavioral studies were among the many forms of experimental testing researchers conducted on people whose genetic characteristics were said to be undesirable (e.g., Blacks, gays and, largely, the disabled).

Another example of experimental testing in America is a well-known test case. The Tuskegee experiment took place early in the twentieth century. It would last 40 years, ending in 1972. Approximately 400 Black American males were infected with syphilis in 1932. The men were left untreated so researchers could investigate the long-term effects of syphilis in the family environment. Most of the men who were investigated died prematurely. The longest surviving members of the Tuskegee experiment lived until 1972. The United States continues to conduct experiments on its private citizens. Harriet Washington wrote a book entitled Medical Apartheid: The Dark History of Medical

Experimentation on Black Americans from Colonial Times to the Present. Many of the stories were revealing: In places like Baltimore, Maryland, children were left untreated for lead paint poisoning in order to collect data.

So long as Whites continue to define Western technology by machines and systems used to advance or forward their personal cause, there can be no movement forward toward true progress. Whites can only return human society to an earlier or less developed state of existing. We've already lived through chattel slavery, two eugenic movements, racial segregation, prejudice and discrimination, and extended periods of vulnerability. So why would Western society choose to disadvantage the remaining world? Why are they choosing to separate from other races of the world? It's their arrogance.

The Arrogant Nature
of Whites

Advancement in Western technology is deeply rooted in arrogance and dangerous aggression. Whites have always been aggressors. They are proudly contemptuous and show great disregard for others. Have you ever heard of the saying, "Praise the lord and pass the ammunition?" Well, such arrogance is said to have come from a United States Navy Chaplin who sanctioned World War II as a religious war. And, "How did the war end," you ask?

World War II ended when the United States detonated not one but two nuclear weapons over the Japanese cities of Hiroshima and Nagasaki. The United

States claimed the Japanese were so aggressive that detonating one bomb over Japan would be futile. They also wanted to send a message to the Soviets who instigated the war. Yet, one question has always remained: Was it necessary to cause that level of death and destruction just to bring an end to the war?

Whites pride themselves on having religious rights to rule the world. They justify intergroup conflict against various races as religious battles or holy wars. Such arrogance becomes quite obvious when White people use religion to take unfair advantage of developing countries. It becomes more obvious when Whites use religion as a catalyst to bring war to foreign countries. Many countries will become obsessed with militarization even before becoming westernized. And the push to militarize a country often changes its understanding of civilization.

Developing countries often come to consider weapons of mass destruction as a consequence of civilization. What they fail to understand is that technology is not always the result of civilization, at least, not civilized or moral thinking. Nor is it always the result of progress. Technology has to benefit the world as a whole in order for it to be considered progress. Depending on the type of technology, it can be a sign that a society has digressed or, perhaps, is moving backward in time.

Technology can advance any group of people obsessed with materialism. But, that doesn't mean they are civilized or part of a civilization. Machinery, equipment, and the application of tools and devices can be found in less developed environments where systems are in place.

More often, these uncivilized environments, societies if you will, can remain culturally stagnant by not developing in more socially acceptable ways. So where does that leave progress?

It leaves progress to countries seeking to advance humanity. As for developing countries in search of military power, progress becomes an effort to obtain Western technology. Many countries in pursuit of Western technology become dependent on Western nations to maintain a strong military presence. It's the inability of developing countries to mimic Western nations that leads White people to believe they have surpassed other races in intellect, achievement, and ability.

When we look beyond superiority complexes or racial stereotypes and consider impactful experiences, the context in which race matters, and certain beliefs about race, we find out that race does matter in understanding the nature of relationships. Consider one's feelings of anger. Whites are more likely to show anger toward different races, especially Blacks, when they believe they have been challenged. In this regard, Whites are more likely to turn their anger into aggression than nonwhites.

Stereotypes about different races are more likely to occur in contexts that underscore the importance of social roles and relationships. For example, nonwhites are more likely than Whites to talk about having social encounters with people that include universal interaction. In addition, nonwhites are more likely to express optimism and joy than Whites when asked about the nature of their relationship or interactions with different racial groups, especially when communicating with family and friends.

Beliefs about stereotypes play an important role in understanding how intergroup relations work in the real world. For example, nonwhites are more likely to agree with the belief that Whites should adapt to racial diversity. But when reporting on their own feelings, more nonwhites than Whites report feelings of frustration about diversity. Nonwhites often make self-reports that tend to be consistent with cultural stereotypes as if the individual person compares himself or herself to a cultural standard when thinking of a response, for example, I am Black; therefore, I must be inferior. Or, I am Black; therefore, I must be unintelligent.

On a special note of importance: Intelligence is universal. Therefore, no one race can truly be superior to others in intelligence. Unfortunately, aggression is not. Evolution conditioned Whites to be arrogantly aggressive. And they have assumed control, power, and authority over most of the planet as a result.

Regardless of how dominant Whites are in the Western world, they should not try to impose their culture on another. Whites have an obligation to adopt developing countries while remaining objective in ways that do not unfairly portray any particular one. They also have an obligation to share technological advancements and break-throughs that develop from interacting with countries once international agreements are reached.

In the second half of this chapter, we discussed the arrogant nature of Whites to include their motivation behind Western Technology. In this chapter, we also briefly considered two different paths of civilization and how technology can hinder progress. In chapter 4, we will consider Whites and their proclivity for racism, revealing a cascade of fascinating events that underlie their thoughts, emotions, and actions. These events often take place over the course of global history.

Chapter 4
Their Proclivity for Racism

McGuire, 2022

Among the many misdeeds of British rule in India, history
will look upon the Act which deprived a whole nation of
arms as the blackest.

Mahatma Gandhi

First, I was hesitant to cite a quote by Gandhi, a man many
people said was less than ordinary, let alone extraordinary.
A champion of cause for the people of India, yet, Gandhi
was coarse or crude in his lack of compassion for the
suffering of Black people, which often included his desire
to help. Still, his message serves an important purpose
today. It is a testament that shows Europeans and their
proclivity for racism as part of the European will to
conquer. Although Gandhi's harsh or rough tone toward
Black people made him deserving of the most serious
criticism—as a continuation of the European will to
conquer—he believed the British were extremely
dishonorable people.

This chapter is a continuation of the European will
to Conquer. Therefore, I will explain more about Europeans
and their proclivity for racism. So, take this time to regroup
and then enjoy some of the many fascinating and varied
reasons why Europeans have these natural racist
tendencies.

Natural Racist Tendencies

We've been dealing with the problem of racism forever and a day. Most people have been accused of bigotry, hypocrisy, or the like. Their attitudes or belief system is thought to be a normal part of human evolution. However, the European will to conquer is endeavored by their proclivity for racism.

Proclivity is a natural tendency to behave in characteristic ways. Europeans and their proclivity for racism are forged by the extreme conditions of prehistoric Europe. It is also reinforced by an excessive need for admiration. Their behavior can be explained by using the Cress Theory created by Dr. Frances Cress Welsing. In the Cress Theory, Dr. Welsing believes Europeans have a need to be the object of high regard. It developed from having a fear of being a numerical minority on the planet. Further, many Europeans are uncomfortable about their genetically recessive traits. The problem here is that Europeans believe they will experience genetic annihilation if they continue to interbreed with various races on the planet. As a result, they behave in ways that do not take into consideration the relative nature of others.

Europeans have a need or tendency to insert themselves into areas of history that took place long before their evolution. A fine example of the European need for admiration can be seen in the classic film Cleopatra: Queen. American actress Elisabeth Taylor played the iconic role of Cleopatra. For decades, Hollywood covered up the truth about the racial identity of Cleopatra to prevent

Europeans from experiencing jealousy, grief, and resentment.

In the film, it was obvious Cleopatra was White. But in actuality, she was a very dark skinned African. Granted, Rome and Greece were thriving at that time. And Cleopatra was in constant contact with the Roman Empire. Nevertheless, she was African.

Even today, whenever you conduct an Internet-based search on Cleopatra, she is identified as European with Greek ancestry. The Hollywood box office block buster, released June 12, 1963, is recorded in history as one of the most famous and powerful love stories ever to grace the big screen.

Today, Europeans continue to rewrite history by whitewashing it in an organized effort to conceal the unpleasant truth. The truth is Europeans are the most recent race to evolve. Therefore, they cannot claim any discoveries, inventions, or scientific breakthroughs without first recognizing or acknowledging the many contributions Africans made to the world, especially in the context of art, culture, and science. Europeans and their resentment toward the teachings of African people—even before their presence in early Europe—is the main reason why they developed a strong proclivity for racism.

All proclivities, be the behavioral outcome racism, sexism, aggression, or something else, such as jingoism or ethnocentrism, are based on the natural tendency to behave in characteristic ways. These ways are stereotypical in nature and can be harmful or helpful in assigning people to a particular category. Stereotypes help to simplify the complexity of relationships that exist among people in the real world. When we assign a label to someone like racist, it becomes easy to ignore or disregard a relationship with that person. In fact, once a label is assigned to a person, it becomes much harder to embrace him or her even when confronted with contradictory evidence.

The intentions of a racial stereotype are completely clear in meaning thus unable to be misunderstood. A racial stereotype is meant to mischaracterize people. Therefore, it often brings harm to a person's public image. For example, there is no ambiguous response when we call someone dumb, stupid, or unintelligent. Everyone is completely clear about the nature of meaning or intention.

Racial stereotypes are unambiguous in the face of European progress. For example, as early as 332BC, King Alexander or Alexander the Great showed how spiteful his intentions were toward the Egyptians by destroying Egyptian monuments, statues, and artifacts. Egypt failed to recover most of their history as a result of the Greek invasion.

When European (Greek) expeditions were deployed to Egypt, its members were filled with awe as they gazed at the number of monuments built in recognition of Black Pharaohs. These monumental figures were incontestably Black as the shape of their nose gave away their identity. King Alexander destroyed the noses of many statues to spite Egyptians, an African people devoted to ancient Egyptian practices and loyal to the ancient Pharaohs or the Egyptian Gods. He strongly believed the Egyptians were pagan people and lacked intelligence. Therefore, King

Alexander wanted to colonize Egypt to make way for European progress.

After Alexander established the capital of Egypt, a city that bore his name, he also developed plans to build a great Library. Dedicated to the Muses, the Library of Alexandria was constructed in around 295BC, after Alexander's death. His death occurred during the reign of his successor Ptolemy I Soter (some scholars say it was during the reign of Ptolemy II Philadelphus 285–246BC).

Today, people can see the consequence of European progress simply by conducting an Internet-based Boolean search for "sphinx, shot, and nose" on any search engine. We gain a better understanding of their resistance when we attempt to retrieve information on history such as, "Who shot off the Sphinx nose?" Europeans refuse to accept re-sponsibility or take ownership for perpetuating misinform-ation that continues to render the world culturally ignorant. According to Google, it was:

> Muhammad Sa'im al-Dahr, a Sufi Muslim from the khanqah of Sa'id al-Su'ada in 1378, who found the local peasants making offerings to the Sphinx in the hope of increasing their harvest and therefore defaced the Sphinx…

Today, Black people are filled with awe as they gaze at the ruins of massive Egyptian monuments. It is a feeling of amazement and respect for Egypt mixed with sadness and disgust for European invaders that is often coupled with a feeling of learned helplessness. The world is extremely complex, and Europeans have the ability to inspire dread or reverence. Instead, they choose to inspire dread by embracing their proclivity for racism.

Once upon a time, most people openly embraced racism. Well, it appears that the world has come full circle. Racism is again becoming increasingly common. And more people are openly willing to embrace it. People no longer hide racism behind conservatism. Politicians are running for public office while openly embracing racism. People are no longer using conservatism as an endearing quality to uphold xenophobic beliefs and traditions. In the past, anyone who showed consideration for racism was passed over for election, seen as lacking in moral character. Today, the only thing that matters in an election is finding voters who share your sentiments. You can even stereotype someone and it just doesn't matter.

While racial stereotyping is increasing, it no longer appears to have significant consequences. President Joe Biden is called Jim Crow Joe by many. Yet people continue to find endearing qualities about him. His election to the Oval Office is a testament that stereotypes do not matter. European men in the West are widely believed to be racists, bigots, and hypocrites. European women in the West are considered to be more racist, bigoted, and hypocritical in this day and age than their male counterparts.

For example, *Karen*, a pejorative term used to characterize a White woman perceived as entitled or privileged, demanding cultural respect beyond what is deserving. Her tears appear to be what affects the racial dynamics or shapes the change-producing forces behind the

European will to conquer. Further, it has been the motivation behind Black lynchings since chattel slavery.

It appears that Europeans in developed countries perceive themselves as more driven or motivated to conquer than are those in less developed countries. This perception makes since. In more highly developed countries, there is a greater chance of multiculturalism, more social interaction, and as racial equality or racial equity increases, racial stereotypes will probably diminish.

Europeans are more likely than nonwhites to perceive differences among racial groups. Even in the absence of race, the characteristics of racism remains ever present. Jingoism and ethnocentrism are natural tendencies to consider someone's ethnic group more important than strangers and others. There is a comparison we can use in the story of Moses from the King James Version Christian Bible. It begins with Numbers chapter 12:

> Miriam and Aaron began to talk against Moses because of his Cushite wife, for he had married a Cushite. ... The anger of the LORD burned against them, and he left them. When the cloud lifted from above the tent, Miriam's skin was leprous—it became as white as snow. Aaron turned toward her and saw that she had a defiling skin disease. ...

Here, I refute the racial origins of Moses by explaining it in greater detail. Since the Cushite religion was very similar to the Egyptian religion, it's more likely that religion played a crucial role in the bitterness experienced by Miriam and Aaron as they were Hebrew.

Race should not have factored into the racial equation since all three were African, Moses being a multiethnic African.

The Cushites (the people from the kingdom of Kush) were Ethiopids who Descended from Ethiopia. The fact that Aaron was appalled by the appearance of his wife and her defiling skin disease strengthens earlier conclusions drawn from biblical text. That is to say, the threesome appears to be Black people. Curiously, whenever racism is not present or cannot be clearly defined, we find ourselves engaged in ethnic disputes that mimic racism. Whenever there are competition groups, competing over sources, there is a natural tendency to exert superiority over one another.

European Progress and
the Assertion of White
Supremacy

Today, Europeans are the dominant race throughout most of the world. They control who records history, a motivation that makes them feel superior as a people. The problem is they've rewritten world history to make their people look superior to the remaining world. Many racial groups are in the process of undoing the damage. Only, there are so many defense mechanisms in place designed to help encourage White behavior that they look good or right when judged by the standards of society. One of these defense mechanisms is anthropology.

First, anthropology is no stranger to racism. Its entire premise was centered on using race as a biological marker to justify Eugenics in a historical movement to establish White supremacy. Although today it is mainly concerned with the development and betterment of humanity, it attempted to correct its wrongs by denying the very concept of race and for good reasons. The very idea that humans are separate and distinct races is the brainchild of Carl Linnaeus also known as the father of modern taxonomy.

But, it was Johann Friedrich Blumenbach who grouped humans into five racial categories. Blumenbach also adopted Carl Linnaeus' system of human taxonomy as the basis of moral classification for human intelligence. Whites were viewed as the highest in human intelligence while Black people were considered distastefully inferior in intelligence thus lacking sophistication, regarded as unusual for humans.

For some people, the problem of slavery is inconsequential. They understand that many societies had some form of slavery that was practiced. And, how right they are! For many countries, slavery was the result of war. Winners took the losers hostage. As a result, hostages were often put to work as indentured servants or slaves. However, American chattel slavery was a new evil. It differed from other forms of slavery in that Europeans turned it into a trade profession. Europeans used business companies in the exchange of humans. Blacks were used as commercial goods and products while they provided them as public entertainment and personal services. American slavery also differed in the way a person was enslaved, in the length of servitude, the type of treatment the enslaved endured, and the way in which they were to be viewed (i.e., subhuman).

Blumenbach's research on racial classification would become the basis of anthropological research. Further, due to the research he conducted, the business of slave trading would provide the foundation for slavery to function as a global economic power-base, which fueled the world economy. His research would also justify the continuation of chattel slavery until the end of the Civil War (1865). More importantly, his conception of race gave way to scientific racism, a pseudoscientific practice that continues to maintain a stranglehold on modern-day race research.

The idea that man invented the concept of race is the very reason why so many people would like to dismiss it. However, to do away with the concept of race allows Europeans to cloak their true identity in racial secrecy. The very denial of biological differences among various races also relieves the European from assuming personal responsibility for causing excessive harm to strangers and others. The fact is the word race may serve a practical purpose.

The concept of race was first used in anthropology to categorize breeds of animals. It was later applied to humans when Europeans discovered the concept of whiteness which, until the 16 hundreds, had little to no value in public domains. It was only after Europeans realized that race could be used as a biological marker for humans did the idea of whiteness become important. That much is true.

However, grouping people into categories based on race, or for any reason for that matter, is a basic human function. It was recorded as early as ancient Egypt when the Pharaohs first grouped people into categories of either Jew or Gentile. People are often grouped by category when new information becomes too much to process at a given time. The entire idea of grouping people is for the individual person to learn whether strangers are good people and worthy of consideration regardless of what is officially or outwardly declared to be their situation (as in apartheid, slavery, or prison incarceration, for example).

Further, the concept of grouping people by racial category is said to give the individual person greater freedom of choice or greater competency in decision-making when deciding the nature of new relationships. The problem begins when people fail to compare their opinions with other group members who have considered it and other possible choices. Their failure to make a proper decision or make a good judgment about strangers and others often becomes defensive to them.

European Progress as
a Defense Mechanism

We often refer to European progression as positive development. But, such progress are defense mechanisms used as corrective measures to restore or fix problems created by Europeans who have a natural tendency to cause excessive suffering. A prime example of European progress is the use of science, television and network mediums, and the Internet, which are somewhat reliable due to the iota of truth they tell. This iota of truth is just enough progress to keep the world from existing on the brink of catastrophe, especially catastrophic events that lead to great loss of life.

These mediums are false profits. Some alter our perceptions. Others distort our perspectives. Still more change our impressions based on what we observe or think. In fact, the intended purpose of these mediums is to give the appearance of Europeans as having greater morals and values than in reality. This way, when they're judged by the standards of the individual or society at large, they appear to be morally righteous, good, or just.

A prized example of a Europeanized version of cultural progress involves a situation created by President Ronald Reagan. Had President Ronald Reagan handled the A.I.D.S. epidemic properly, it would not have spread more quickly and more extensively among the American population than normally expected. Gays and Blacks were the hardest hit, suffering needless loses to their communities. President Reagan, who did not want to alert the public of the potential crisis, only did so after his friend Rock Hudson contracted the disease. It would take decades before science could bring the situation under control. Countless lives were needlessly lost. And when scientists finally made a breakthrough in the A.I.D.S. epidemic, Europeans across the world called it progress. Even the onset of the outbreak was needless and senseless.

A medical doctor from Johns Hopkins University wanted a safe environment to investigate the disease. A male airplane steward from Baltimore, Maryland already contracted A.I.D.S. Not understanding the dynamics of relationships between Whites and Blacks, the doctor thought he could contain it. At best, he thought only the Black community would suffer the immediate impact of which there would be a brief period of quarantine for Baltimore City residents. By sending the infected person home, the doctor assumed the person had only limited contact with White people. However, this was not the case.

The steward continued working, moving from state-to-state, flight-after-flight, night-after-night. He had numerous relationships with flight attendants, pilots and their spouses, and other people, both male and female, in various states across the country. The infected person had no idea how bad his situation was. After all, the doctor allowed him to leave the hospital on his own accord. The spread of the disease caused a national outbreak that reached epidemic proportions. Needless to say, the situation could have been prevented. Even after realizing his mistake, the doctor modestly allowed the steward to continue his sexual encounters. Why? He thought the steward only infected Blacks in his community.

It's unfortunate that most people, not just Europeans, have a natural tendency to preserve their own individual wellness and interests, especially when perceived to be valued more than other people. Although the scientific breakthrough was successful in helping reduce the physical impact of the epidemic, it was a corrective measure used to bring the spread of the disease under control. Sadly, it enabled scientists to say, "We're making progress! We've addressed the situation and now have it under control." Remember, President Reagan was okay with the spreading of the A.I.D.S. virus until it affected his friend Rock Hudson. Before then, it was thought to have impacted only gay and Black communities. Again, another preventable event had it not been for Europeans and their self-serving values. Also, the actions of the medical doctor spoke volumes against Europeans and their racial proclivities for progress.

Most Victorians believed in progress. They began to look back and celebrate early European art and culture as a way of reaching higher standards. They praised the Greeks and Romans publicly by celebrating their greatest gifts: their teachings. Today, world cultures are challenging historical facts and evidence to the contrary. It was recently brought to the attention of Europeans that certain aspects of early European history are wrong, a mentally painful moment for them.

Greek and Roman gifts are essentially African, a cultural legacy left to the people of Europe by the Egyptians. After centuries of teaching misinformation to the world, contradictory information is being removed from history and in certain cases revised in a way that further distorts history. In the revising of history, Europeans say they're making steps toward progress. The point is the world is being confronted with European defiance. Not one of these actions is corrective. In fact, their actions further contradict history. There is an old quote spoken by Malcolm X, a classic. It says:

> If you stick a knife in my back nine inches and pull it out six inches, there's no progress. If you pull it all the way out, that's not progress. The progress is healing the wound that the blow made.

In the case of Europeans, they stuck the proverbial knife in our back another six inches and then said they're making progress. In fact, if Brother Malcolm was alive today, he might even point out that European progress, which is the White man's conception of hope, is quickly becoming an inadequate defense for establishing healthy intergroup relations, bettering society, or reaching a state of greater civilization. He may even agree that *European progress* is a corrective measure, which is used as compensation for self-interest.

Using the excuse, "We're making progress. We're moving in the right direction by taking corrective actions to improve the situation. ..." regardless of how steady the answer is, it's quickly becoming an inadequate defense in the general advance of human society. Even when the United States government tries to make amends to Black Americans, they award them with trivial gestures to pacify them. They award Black people with national holidays to pacify them. They elect well-spoken, charismatic politicians in office just to talk about awarding Black Americans reparations so they can pacify them. As a matter of fact, every effort the government makes to compensate Black people is another method they use to pacify them. That's why European progress is nothing more than a corrective measure used to compensate nonwhites. It essentially shows a lack of remorse for the criminal wrongdoings they commit during the initial goal of reaching a state of greater achievement.

Progress does not happen as a result of improving a nation's last performance, either. To further progress or make improvements, there must be an exchange that adds value to humanity as a whole (i.e., the healing must begin). If not, our efforts will be lost or will worsen the quality, value, or strength of humanity.

I am hopeful that by now you can appreciate the progress made in this book. It is a logical derivation of older propositions. Such propositions are derived by explicit assumptions and previously proven propositions. For example, when scientists develop ideas or concepts from a historical origin, we say they derived their conclusions from important sources. In this next chapter, we will turn our attention to value judgments where someone's worth, appropriateness, or importance is determined on the basis of personal beliefs, opinions, or prejudices opposed to the facts.

CHAPTER 5
Value Judgments

> We've been talking about this for a good while, the immorality of drones, dropping bombs on innocent people. It's been over 200 children so far. These are war crimes.
>
> Cornel West

Dr. Cornel West once asked what the United States knows about a military coup that took place in Honduras (2009). He wanted to know was there a connection? He imposed another question: Why did the US drone strike on countless innocent lives not matter to millions of people here in the United States? How many children died needlessly and senselessly to preserve freedom or protect the integrity of Americans? For that matter, I'm asking why? Inquiring minds would like to know.

The questions Dr. West asked were at one point addressed directly to President Barack Obama who some people felt made poor judgments due to his inexperience in office. While Obama tried to remain politically correct in his approach to handling world affairs, Brother Cornel reminded him of how it contributed to the needless and senseless suffering of others.

As you can see, he was profoundly critical of President Obama given all the crimes committed by the corporate elite. In fact, Obama bailed out Wall Street executives when in only 16 months, they stole 16 trillion hard earned, taxpaying American dollars. Yet, not one was made to endure prison. Not one was questioned for their lack of resignation and quickly letting go moral principles and professional ethics in the great Wall Street heist.

On the other hand, Tanya McDowell received a five-year prison sentence for sending her son to school in a better school district. Curiously, Felicity Huffman received a prison sentence of 14 days. She paid to have her daughter's SAT scores inflated. Today, and one of many, Felicity's court case has come to be known as the college-admissions cheating scandal. As Cornel investigates the nature of moral thinking, his question to politicians like Obama is where's the moral dilemma in your sense of judgment, bailing out greedy Wall Street executives whose unscrupulous nature made it impossible for Tanya McDowell to afford decent schooling for her only child. Cornel's provocative views on moral identity development continue to generate considerable controversy. Critics continue to challenge his controversial views on President Obama. Today, both gentlemen continue to show their differences of opinion on a wide range of political topics.

Mark Twain once said, "It is a difference of opinion that makes horses race." In other words, differences of opinion are based on value judgments. Value judgments occur when someone determines the truthfulness, usefulness, or importance of others on the basis of personal beliefs, opinions, or prejudices rather than pointing to the facts. People have a natural tendency to place their needs or desires before those of others. However, those of us who continue to hold our integrity consider their lack of morals indefensible or unethical. Integrity cuts across grains of culture. That's why our discussion on value judgments has bearing on the United States and how it performs against the rest of the world.

We can see that the United States places its needs or desires before those of others. We can also see it when government officials make value judgments against foreign nations. Upon freeing a country from the tyranny of oppression, America often liberates it of its precious land, minerals, and important resources. It's readily witnessed when government officials attempt to make amends by providing citizenship to members of war-torn countries after its people helped America win foreign wars. Many countries fear the United States as a result.

People from around the world call the United States a Godless country. Why? It continues to create the worst scenarios that life can bring. First, let's not forget why Saddam Hussein was assassinated. He certainly wasn't assassinated for humanitarian reasons.

Saddam was a byproduct of the Central Intelligence Agency (CIA). When he tried to establish independence from the Agency (i.e., he sought to control important resources needed for Western survival), the United States ordered his assassination. In order to mask negative responses from the public, the United States convicted Saddam for crimes against humanity. And why was Mu'ammar Al-Gaddafi killed?

Gaddafi was a Libyan revolutionary. He certainly was not killed because of his status as an African dictator. Gaddafi wanted to empower African nations. He created a new African economic system supported by the Gold-based Dinar, which would back African currency, creating African independence from European and Western currencies. With the endorsement of Western imperialists,

Mu'ammar Al-Gaddafi was assassinated October 20, 2011 in Sirte, Libya.

Even Nigeria went as far as asking Communist Russia for protection against the United States in fear that it would rape, pillage, and plunder the country's wealth and resources. Other governments call the United States a terrorist organization because most of its value judgments against foreign powers are made on the basis of personal beliefs, opinions, or prejudices contrary to the facts. Regardless, America is constantly putting its concerns and interests before those of others, which show a lack of remorse. That's why the White man's conception of hope is socially inadequate as a goodwill gesture. He is insincere. And, his insincerity comes from being an individual.

Where did the concept of individualism come from? Is there any such concept as an individual in a world that is becoming increasingly interdependent? Let's see!

Individualism

The concept of individualism started with the nomadic practices of early Europeans. It was born during age of nomadism when the Cro-Magnon conducted massive raids throughout Europe, often settling in areas they invaded. All over the world, early Europeans raped, pill-aged, and plundered their way throughout the course of history. It is a part of European behavior; an aggression learned or adopted from the early nomadic practices of prehistoric Europe. The concept of rugged individualism comes from that very idea. As well, that's why America is an individualistic society and not a collective one. America evolved from the moral thoughts of early Europeans. As a result, it teaches meritocracy as a form of independence. The problem is the age of independence is dying out. We are becoming increasingly interdependent, relying on mutual assistance, support, cooperation, or interaction among a global network of societies, cultures, and people. Therefore, the rugged individual, if he ever existed, died out along with the nomadic practices of the caveman.

Although we can see the rugged nature of modern Europeans—for example, slavery, segregation, and South African apartheid—these systems were put in place because everyone has had help along the road to success, wealth, or power, some fame even stardom. From your parents who reared you until adulthood and the tutor who helped you earn a passing grade during mid-term examinations to the interviewers who took a chance on hiring you due to your work ethics or academic potential, no one on this planet made it in life without the aid of personal assistance, at least, not in this modern day and age.

Individualism and Meritocracy

You probably think you know what it means to be an individual, and like most people, you probably don't consider yourself as one. The fact is each of us thinks of ourselves in meritocratic ways. Why? That's the way America is setup. It is an individualistic society. Therefore, it teaches meritocracy as a source of personal independence.

Individualism teaches meritocracy to people. Under the system of meritocracy, people develop self-serving values rather than collective goals or interests. In fact, the entire idea behind pulling yourself up by your bootstraps hinges on the premise that a person, any person, who tries hard enough, can make it according to his or her own admission. And that whosoever fails to make it in Western society is maladaptive. The notion that Northern and Western societies continue to exist so individuals can achieve without constraint from government interventions or without having to follow collective interests comes from the idea of individualism or meritocracy.

Meritocracy is propaganda taken to the extreme in Western nations. The idea behind the myth of meritocracy is the reason why people have such misguided views about race, class, and culture in America. For example, it leads people to believe that they're in the position they're in because of poor work ethnics. Where am I going with this? Well, if I am taught to believe in personal merit as every red-blooded American has been taught, it then becomes reasonable for me to believe that America is a country that gives opportunities and advantages to people based on their ability rather than their wealth or inherent rights. It also teaches me that the cultural elite are in their positions due to their natural ability to succeed at life. In other words, under a system of meritocracy, I would have no reason whatsoever to think my circumstances was the result of, perhaps, my out-group status position. I would be more inclined to believe that I or any person in my situation was lazy, or perhaps, unintelligent.

In fact, if I considered my situation compared to people who had better circumstances or who live in affluent communities, my reasoning would be reinforced by my own admission. The thought of oppression would be removed from the racial equation by default. The whole process of social stratification would be a matter of ability. Racism, classism, and the more pervasive isms would be justified, again, by my own admission. And using that reasoning, which would not be wrong, I would not have an argument to make. Why? My failure to adapt would be a personal problem and not something systemic.

Curiously, meritocracy suggests that the Western world is colorblind. That if countries like America are left alone, it will correct its own problems and function as it should. But since meritocracy is a colorblind ideology, it actually cannot recognize or identify systemic problems like structural racism.

In a book written by Michael A. Bradley, a reporter once asked Gandhi what he thought about Western civilization. Gandhi replied, "I think it would be a good idea." As with any individualistic society, there can be no movement forward toward a state of greater civilization. There can only be a steady source of regression to an earlier and less developed way of behaving or a generally worse state. I caught a glimpse at this form of regression under the totalitarian rule of Russia or centralized governmental systems where the driving force behind it is communism, such as Northern Viet Cong and, certainly,

European progression and the Western man's need for global conquest.

We now have interest groups lobbying to influence political policies for their own personal gain while individuals by and large struggle to achieve standard healthcare. Soon, most of the world will be governed by one or more small groups. Before long, and this is the ultimate goal of interest groups, a few members will achieve Oligarchy status. The main goal of most Oligarchs is to create a system of government in which they hold power and control the world's economy. And that's the entire premise behind the games they play.

European Progression
as a Source of Pride

Europeans take pride in their progression. They take great pride in their achievements, acclaims, and accomplishments. And rightfully so! Each succession is a part of achieving a goal or reaching a higher standard of progression. There should be a deep sense of pride whenever anyone achieves something special that other people have not. After all, it's only natural.

Europeans are profoundly ethnocentric, which fosters in a great sense of pride in their own people. Pride also reduces the urge to attain and maintain a positive self-image. One thing we've recently considered about European pride is the understanding that it has blossomed. Europeans have group pride, gay pride, and western pride. The British become more prideful in their appearance while the Irish take pride in their Irish heritage. But the one thing odd or peculiar about such pride is how preoccupied proud Europeans are with discrimination.

Throughout American history, Southern White men said they must preserve the innocence of Southern White women. White men spend an inordinate amount of time discriminating or victimizing others as a source of pride in their women. Could it be that pride is a prehistoric source of aggression for the White man. After all, Freudian psychoanalytic theory suggests pride, as part of our psyche, is a primitive source of instinctive impulses and drives that's always claiming and demanding recognition. In other words, might the White man's source of pride be an aggression that masks important bouts of inferiority?

A Source of Pride

I guess a good question would be why has European progress taken the world in a direction motivated by activities that are extremely detrimental to humans? Again, it's their pride!

Europeans gave the world nuclear, radiological, chemical, and biological warfare, and the hydrogen bomb, all resulted from European technology. Europeans take great pride in their weapons of mass destruction. For them it's a necessary evil. In fact, it's a classic example of how technology is mistaken for true progress. It's also an example of how people can mistake technological advancements as a sign of civilization.

Technology can move societies in various directions: toward war or peace, for example. Not all societies are civilized by definition. And not all civilized societies are technologically advanced. These weapons of mass destruction or any weapon that kills, or has the ability to bring significant harm to massive amounts of people, properties, or natural structures, give special insight into the mindset of humans as a whole. Why? Europeans aren't the only race using weapons of mass destructions. But, I fear, their reason for using them may differ.

A great question to explore would be how do weapons of mass destruction solve world problems? One country develops weapons to conquer. Another country develops its arsenal as a matter of self-defense. Yet, a third country develops more weapons of mass destruction to defend itself from the potential threat of foreign powers. So where does it end? It does appear that Europeans are so driven by conquest that they're absolutely determined to control the world by force of arms, regardless of consequences.

Since the rise of Europeans, there appears to be no way we can reduce their aggression to achieve peace. So far, all efforts to reduce violence against Black people have been futile. We're well into the new millennium and White police abuse continues to spark conflict and hatred between Whites and Blacks. Such is the grounds for some of history's greatest moments: When the Supreme Court ruled in favor of racial integration, America was at the height of the Civil Rights movement. When Abraham Lincoln ended chattel slavery in the United States, America was in a Civil

War. And in May of 1970, when the Aborigine Queen ended racism and racial discrimination for her people, indigenous life in Australia was classified as plants and natural fauna. Again, Europeans are, in some way, overcompensating for their shortcomings by masking feelings of inferiority with bouts of supremacy.

Do you remember when I said European progress is taken to the extreme in Western nations? Well, this is what I'm talking about. It's their sense of pride. That's right! European pride in their progress has led to Western expansion and globalization. The reality is the world's becoming a unified whole, grounded in a single principle. Regardless of how the world feels about it, the globalization process is forcing racial and ethnic identity groups to embrace social cohesion, which gives considerable control to the cultural elite at the expense or consideration of others.

As a result, instead of countries voting on whether its societies should be monistic or pluralistic, Western expansion or globalization is setting the tone for countries everywhere. It seems to me that Europeans can take pride in knowing each and every country on the planet is, in some way, trying to mimic the lifestyles of Northern and Western nations. Some people may not see it. But the ultimate goal is for the cultural elite, and only them, to rule, and to rule against all odds. Proud moments for Europeans, right? Wrong! That type of pride flies in the face of humanity. Why? Their haughty attitude about European progression, often expressed unjustifiably, makes them feel superior to others. And such pride creates envy.

Developing countries began to compete against each other. Most strive to be more Western while other countries envy them their success. The rest of the world also begins to follow the pattern of Western progress. The result is a mundane and monistic world influence. For example, developing countries have become a home away from home for European tourism. These countries began to cater to tourism for any European looking for a quick getaway but who wants all the comforts of home. Often, you can't tell one country from the other. These countries are a great source of pride for White people as many are measures of Western culture or European progression. The world is looking bleak.

No longer does the European vacation have the ability to acculturate people. That is to say, many countries that participate in tourism no longer have the potential to change people's cultural attitude and thinking through social contact. It is part of the social impact that European progress has on globalization. More and more developing countries people travel to are starting to look like Europe and North America. And thanks to the World Wide Web, the people are quickly becoming westernized. This means small countries are adopting the cultural attitudes of the Western mainstream.

For example, once people begin to see the potential behind commercialism, they change their country or culture to accommodate the people of Europe and North America. Unfortunately, just like in the Western hemisphere, people become obsessed with profit-making. Their views of gambling become more positive. They become obsessed with consumerism, and then change their laws, customs, practices, or beliefs so that it resembles or are replaced by the practice of its European or North American counterparts.

Now that's not to say countries such as Republic of California and Kingdom of Hawaii were not forced to accommodate Western occupation. Immigrants set up a plantation economy to grow sugar almost immediately after colonial occupation in Hawaii. Laborers from Japan, China, and the Philippines were brought in droves to work in the fields. The native population became victim to disease brought in by Europeans.

Members of Hawaii's branch of government— whose main political motive were often self-advancement and whose methods were unscrupulous—amended the constitution to accommodate Western imperialism, binding important powers invested in the people. In essence, Hawaiians were disadvantaged. And in 1959, the islands of Hawaii became the 49th state of America. With those exceptions, developing countries are willfully reflecting the ugly habits of Western culture.

Undeniably, Europeans understand both the negative and positive consequences of globalization. Global interdependence, totalitarianism, and communalism, removes certain rights of the individual. Perhaps, it's devised to protect the individual from making poor moral decisions. After all, individuals independently make moral decisions.

We're in trouble! It's important for us to understand that we're teetering on the brink of destruction. We're at the very edge of a cliff where human society continues to believe the world is flat. And it just may be. We are transitioning from Capitalism in order to take necessities from the many to accommodate the few. It's the nature of moral thought to settle a difference of opinion so that it becomes acceptable to all those involved. The problem is monistic cultures (perhaps, monocultures) often remove any chances of diversifying moral thinking. In this way, the world is changing to adapt to a new situation; and, it doesn't look promising.

There is a problem with the world when people cannot see that Western nations are moving human society in a contradictory direction. The problem is people are taught to view life through the aesthetic lens of White male supremacy. Even as readers proof through the content in this book, as a result of European influencing, they will find much of the new information difficult to accept even if it is promoted as socially acceptable or considered to be of higher standard. Why? Europeans continue to make every effort to maintain control of history as a way to prevent their people from recognizing or accepting blame, guilt, suspicion, or doubt.

Europeans actively seek to control the narrative so they do not have to experience dissonance. After all, dominant society decides, to a large extent, what aspects of life are most important. Their priority is to ensure that little Bill and Penny Annie are not emotionally scarred by shame and doubt.

Interestingly, I've learned that Blacks in highly developed countries perceive themselves as more similar to Whites than do Whites who live in the same countries.

Perhaps, it's a difference of opinion. But, might the way we socialize produce differences in how we come to consider one another? A person would seem to think that in more highly developed countries, people from every walk of life would share similarities due to better education and careers, and as racial equality increases, so should stereotypes diminish. One might think. Truth of the matter is nondominant cultural groups are more likely than dominant cultural groups to perceive similarity between the races.

We've considered many aspects of value judgments to include individualism and meritocracy. Here, my goal in this chapter is to convince readers that selfish ambitions will only lead to cultural regressions, especially reversions to earlier, less complicated generations of civilization, perhaps, associated with paganism or hedonism. Also, in this chapter and throughout the book, I attempt to explore the motivation behind European progression. It is not a sketchy explanation based solely on theory but empirical evidence upon which people readily agree. In the next chapter, we will try to understand why Europeans are so willful in their ignorance to bring harm to others. There, we will have a deep discussion about European diehards who continue to hold out to the bitter end.

CHAPTER 6
Willful Ignorance

McGuire, 2022

> In Rhodesia a white truck driver passed a group of idle natives and muttered, "They're lazy brutes." A few hours later he saw natives heaving two-hundred-pound sacks of grain onto a truck, singing in rhythm to their work. "Savages," he grumbled. "What do you expect?"
>
> Gordon W. Allport (1958)

Although Gordon W. Allport intended for the opening passage to speak on the nature of prejudice, it is a prime example of how Europeans willfully and openly embrace racism. And, it is that level of willfulness that drives the European will to conquer.

The father of social psychology, Gordon Allport once said prejudice can be extinguished through the use of education or information. However, he never spoke directly to the intentions of diehards who stubbornly resisted change, yielding to the nature of Europeans. Those who stubbornly or willfully seek to harm strangers and others, while resisting specific opinions or advice from members of their own racial group, are in fact racists. It's their willful ignorance that keeps them from understanding certain facts or truths necessary for the establishment of healthy intergroup relations.

Relationships are based on value, worth, or mutual esteem. These significant feelings allow people to form important connections needed to regard another or others in very specific ways. This valuation is specific to the task of judging or estimating someone's importance, worth, or usefulness. Willful ignorance is specific in his or her intentions, especially with the intention of harming somebody or despite knowing it will harm others. For the average racist person, their ignorance is deliberate.

What the racist person lacks in compassion is compounded by self-serving values. Regardless of how bigoted they are, whether they are devoid of a moral compass, in spite of them being indiscreet and unpredict- able people who will likely cause intentional harm or trouble to strangers and others, there is a method to their madness.

Apparently, there is a very good reason for the violent actions of racist individuals. Racists believe they are preserving their inheritance. They believe they're entitled to hereditary ownership of the planet along with its wealth, possessions, and resources. They call the process Western expansion while others refer to it as globalization. The idea is to assimilate entire nations on a global scale or adopt important organizations, especially social institut- ions, on a global scale. Colleges, hospitals, and financial institutions not only reflect our customs and traditions, these well-known establishments define entire nations. Who we are, where we come from, and what we are all about, are defined by our cultural identity.

However, their level of confidence has been shaken by the coexistence of distinct identity groups, groups given the same privileges and opportunities as the European. The very idea of diversity is uncomfortable for Europeans. Many refuse to commit to the act of social inclusion. They feel it poses the greatest threat to their existence. Further, they believe that diversity can create interpersonal conflict among separate and distinct cultural systems due to personal biases and prejudices toward distinct identity groups. They believe it's the promise of compromise that disturbs their very existence. They feel threatened by the idea that certain opportunities will be lost due to ideological practices like diversity or racial integration. For them, the idea of interacting with nonwhites is unappealing.

Europeans refuse to share knowledge with people who do not look like them. Many are completely confident in their own abilities to succeed. However, they are confused as to why they must advocate diversity when the goal has always been to breed out the melanin in nonwhites so they become more European. They believe that diversity will create a degenerate form of higher civilization in the world as they know it.

For the European, his will to conquer has always been to establish a monistic world led or operated by a centralized government. It would rule, unopposed, over every aspect of life. Specifically, the new world order would replace democracy with any system of government where a single political party holds power and, ultimately, controls the economy. Interestingly, every action taken, every step made toward achieving progress, has been a concerted effort to make the world revolve around the European.

For example, President Woodrow Wilson launched a campaign on September 3, 1919 that would attempt to elevate any person who held the office of Commander-in-Chief to the status of world leader. The idea of world leaders accepting Wilson's proposition, The League of

Nations, would be his attempt to bring the entire world under one system of rule.

Had it happened, countries would cooperate with the United States by forming a centralized governmental system as the center for the entire world. As a single party, unopposed, the United States would be free to control the world's social, economical, political, and cultural life. It was America's second attempt at global communism. President Donald Trump and his pirated approach to politics would be a third attempt at operating under totalitarianism and, quite possibly, communism.

The greatest ambition of the White European racist is to rule the world with absolute power. From white-washing history to miseducating the American Negro, European Whites make concerted efforts to exploit their proposed superiority. They make every effort to oppress nonwhites in intelligence, achievement, and natural ability. Europeans often adopt and display attitudes of condescension to any race they perceive to be inferior.

Meanwhile, they dupe the world into believing they're gracious and generous people. Any accusations of supremacy are often defused with generous gestures of forgive-ness. When they're not flaunting their proposed superiority to perceived inferiors, they're giving people the false im-pression that differences between their race and nonwhites are incidental matters of evolution. Their willful ignorance allows them to pretend entire races are not being oppressed or their involvement is not the case.

Europeans and Their Willful Ignorance

Willful ignorance among Europeans occurs when a racist person seeks to avoid civil or criminal liability for his or her wrongdoings by intentionally keeping themselves unaware of facts that would implicate them or render them liable in a court of law. In other words, a racist person can dupe himself or herself into believing he or she is innocent or has been victimized simply by exposing the victim. You already heard about *Karen*, any White woman perceived as entitled or privileged beyond what is right, fair, or just? Just like racism, willful ignorance is multidimensional. So, there are many degrees, secessions, and aggressions to it. What's sad about people who give in to their willful ignorance thus openly embrace racism is how carefully thought out their intentions or motives are.

There are many questions we must consider in order to ascertain some understanding of the "who, what, when, where, why, and how's" of racism. Our best understanding will come from defining various dimensions of racism. But let's not jump to any conclusions at this point. We cannot be sure that any accusation of racism is an open or shut case. Whenever these type-A racist personalities have the ability to make value judgments on the basis of personal beliefs, opinions, or prejudices rather than speak the facts, it helps people decide exactly what is and is not true about racism.

You might like to pay close attention to the actual terms. These terms are so embedded in American culture that each one conveys some aspect of our political beliefs. Hence, you may not consider them to be racists. With that said, not every degree of hatred will lead to open acts of racism even though the intention may be the same.

Conservatism is a dimension of racism. While humans may be little bundles of prejudice, bound by the limitations of experience, it is the willful ignorance of *conservatives* to resist any aspect of change or stubbornly give up certain beliefs, positions, or attitudes. Such ignorance drives the European will to conquer.

There are other dimensions of racism yet to be discussed. Aversion is also a dimension of racism. Much in the same way as conservatism, *aversive racism* is a strong, irrational fear or irrational hatred of change. However, what is interesting here is this type of racism is characterized by avoidance behavior. For example, an aversive racist will avoid strangers and others just to prevent social contact with them. In their minds, if there is no social interaction, then there can be no diversity.

It is easy to understand how someone who is racist can be resistant to change. However, it is nearly impossible to perceive how someone so racist can stubbornly persists in their own beliefs or opinions, especially when it is not beneficial to them and causes deliberate harm to others. However, therein lays the crux of the matter.

Racists are consumed by their hatred toward strangers and others. This, I decree, is their willful ignorance. Racists have feelings of intense hostility toward nonwhites even after learning of their value or worth. What's most notable about racists are the colorful ways in which they will resist change or their stubborn persistence to uphold tradition.

Xenophobia is the last dimension of racism we will discuss. Xenophobes have an intense fear or an irrational dislike of immigrants, refugees, and nonwhites. Does that sound like anyone you may know? Well, the difference in attitude is the irrational fear or hatred xenophobes have toward strangers and others. Every aspect of a stranger's identity is loathed by the xenophobe. From their customs, cultures, and beliefs, the cultural attitude of a xenophobe shows the true nature of racism.

The Nature of Racism

Racism in America started when Europeans developed cultural nihilism as a result of losing the Civil War. Although it wasn't referred to as racism until 1936, it was a social movement in middle nineteenth-century America which sought to bring about social stability to American society by exterminating newly freed Blacks through acts of terrorism and assassination.

At the end of the Civil War, the Confederacy totally rejected established social conventions and beliefs, especially doctrines enabling certain rights and privileges to newly freed Blacks. Many Confederates, to include General Nathan Bedford Forrest, believed there was no objective basis for truth and that Black lives were pointless and their values worthless. It was General Forest and others who believed that the established authority of the Union was corrupt and should be submitted in order to rebuild a just society for the race it was intended.

Forrest's reputation in the Confederate Army and as a Freemason earned him a place among the Ku Klux Klan as the first Grand Wizard. During that time, the Period of Reconstruction (1866 – 1877), General Forrest conducted an eleven-year killing spree, terrorizing the lives of and murdering countless Black Americans. It was the contempt White Americans had for Black lives that often evoked feelings of anger, hostility, or animosity among them. So, what about today? Why the continued aggression with the old diehards holding out to the bitter end?

It's the void! European Whites are experiencing a feeling that comes with loss or privation. In privation, important resources that are essential for human wellness such as food, clothing, and shelter are scarce or lacking. Much like Abraham Maslow and his hierarchy of human motives, when physiological needs are not met, people cannot achieve; and, when safety needs are not met, there can be no need for love and security. Now, I know you understand how the concept works for an individual person. But the question is, "How does it work for an entire population of people?" Is it possible that the basic needs of an entire race are not satisfied and, therefore, cannot achieve higher standards of civilization? And before we re-hash the topic of Western technology and the advancement to Western civilizations, understand that, perhaps, the reason why our society struggles to maintain basic physio-logical needs is essentially because our five main needs have not been satisfied in the proper sequence.

What we, as a nation, even as human society, institutionalize as progress is poorly mistaken for civilization. Progress does not define civilization. Nor do you need technology to achieve progress. Progress is a means to achieving civilization. We've also made quantum leaps in technology, leaps and bounds that block or delay true progress. Even the type of progress made by Europeans and Westerners has very little to do with the true nature of progress. But what is progress anyway?

What we do know is European progress is defined by the rate of production. Rapid production is the hallmark of progress. Production stabilizes the economy. Rapid production advances a society. The economy is motivated by technology, which is a measure of progress. Socialism is a way to control economic progress. Economic progress is the back bone of Capitalism. And, both Capitalism and Communism are fueled by global conquest. As you will see next, progress, as White people understand it, is defined by four means:

- Economic growth or progress.
- Rate of production in which rapid production is the hallmark of European progress.
- Expansion of territories to include the possession of land, minerals, and important resources regardless of collateral damage.
- And technological advancement at the cost to or loss of life.

Unfortunately, the aforementioned have little to nothing to do with true progress. Most European progress has been based on taking corrective actions to rectify problems initially created by some imperfection we made that, as a fault or defect, impacts entire nations. We mentioned the A.I.D.S. epidemic earlier. We're now living in the age of the Corona Virus 2019 strain (COVID-19), the world's worse epidemic. It will be years before we can correct the inactivity that enabled COVID-19 to spread rapidly around the world and at a predicted loss of one third of the total population. In this regard, the world is tired of European nations selling mistakes as advancement or progress.

In another example, a medical doctor uses seven fertilized eggs to impregnate a woman on the premise that one or two eggs will survive. If all eggs survive fertilization, the doctor is forced to terminate the remaining eggs in order for the woman to have a healthy pregnancy. Otherwise, she runs the risk of losing the intended pregnancy. Hence, human society is tired of being lied to.

European Progress and
Western Civilization

The world is tired of being deceived. Western governments continue to deceive the world by distorting information that is systematically spread to promote European progress. As a result, the world is waking up.

The world is growing wise to the European idea of progress. European progress is an effort to correct a problem created when a country puts its own interests, needs, and wishes ahead of others. It becomes problematic when the country deceives developing countries by telling untruths. Therefore, European progress ultimately comes with consequences, which are promoted as a byproduct of Westernization.

When a developing country changes its laws, customs, practices, or beliefs so that it resembles or is replaced by its European or Western counterpart, it's often because modern nations publicize its resources as a way to aid the country in furthering its development. The consequences become obvious when the country's officials realize their people are worse off than intended. Meanwhile, Western nations continue to benefit long after the country is poorly or inadequately supplied with resources.

European progress follows a specific pattern. Modern nations will offer a piece of the ultimate goal, modernization as a measure of trust. First, they sell you on the idea of liberty. Next, they will westernize your country. Then, they liberate it of land, minerals, and natural resources. That would be the plundering. The result is your country suffers needlessly in poverty while European and Western nations steadily benefit or prosper from your country's wealth, especially through fraudulent means during wartime or civil unrest.

And how do you know when your country has been plundered or conquered by the will of Europeans and Westerners? They will offer citizenship to your people as a gesture of goodwill. Government officials will be condescending to you and your people while their citizens arrogantly boast about gaining or acquiring your country's wealth by way of superior strength, skill, or intellect. Even if you're not in direct contact with Europeans and Westerners by and large, the reality of your situation will dawn on you just like someone just took off the blinders from your eyes.

European progress can be defined by the production of Western civilization. In fact, it is what most people refer to as civilization. It is described by cultural and technological development, usually gradual, which enables a nation to reach higher standards or a state of greater civilization. The establishment of most societies is marked by the amount of progress it makes. In Western civilizations, progress is also marked by the development of complex social, economical, and political organizations as well as artistic, scientific, and material possessions.

In the Western world, European progress encourages most societies to advance. Such advancement more often happens in an unrestrained manner, so much so, it's usually regarded as a menace. Rapid development often leads to a quick fix, fast paced society filled with shortcuts and loose ends. Perhaps the greatest difference in Western civilization and societies is the continuous progression that leads to cultural addictions: addictions to work, sex, violence, and more.

Rapid production is the hallmark of European progress. Westernization is known for European progress since Europeans have a strong propensity for it. Now, I'm not talking about their willingness to work or endure manual labor, which we know is not the case. However, the progress is so rapid or the labor is so enduring that it's often mistaken for civilization. Again, civilization is not characterized by progress nor can you make the case that technology is either. Technology is the result of motivation. Motivation begets labor. And labor results in progress. Therefore, motivation is what drives people to make progress.

Societies can be motivated to progress in very specific ways. Societies can be motivated to be dominant or peaceful. If a society is motivated by peace, it may not be consumed by technological advancements that lead to aggression. In fact, societies may not be motivated by aggression or influenced by the results of technology at all. That's not to say technology will not be a part of the civilizing process. It just may not be a priority.

Civilizing processes include a high level of culture, knowledge and sophistication, acquired through education and exposure to fine arts. Most civilized people are characterized by shared beliefs, customs, practices, and social behavior associated with a particular society. People who live in civilizations are more or less bound by a particular place, class, or time to which they belong. As a result, they develop a particular set of attitudes that characterizes certain beliefs in their culture, group, or membership. Civilized people are more often nurtured, especially in order to reflect the advancement of a particular society. What's notable about the civilizing process is how calm, quiet, and free from violence or disturbance civilized people are. European progress occurs to the contrary.

European progress is driven by conquest. As a people, Europeans are compelled by a personal need to suc-ceed. It's not about achieving. They are driven, specifically, by an inner compulsion to exploit, oppress, and humiliate Black people. History tells us that Europeans are driven by an irrational fear or hatred of strangers and others. It has more to do with change in the nature of relationships of power between White and Black people. The problem is White people fear the same exclusionary policy of racial inequality they imposed on Black people throughout their intellectual history. So, they continue to dehumanize and demoralize them. While they are preoccupied with pro-gression (progression being a metaphor for aggression), their inability to experience compassion or to respond emotionally to Black people poses significant problems for the European race. The point is Europeans lack the ability to control their aggression as a result of being driven by irresistible compulsion.

Hypothesizing Criticisms for
Emotional Detachment Theory:
A Contemporary Perspective

Emotional Detachment Theory states that Europe-ans emotionally disengaged or detached themselves from humanity through prehistoric sources of aggression. Both environmental experiences and situational influences of prehistoric Europe are considered the source behind their aggression, racism and sexism. For a minority of re-searchers, this theory fosters a scientific climate for understanding racism. This climate underscores the importance of observing racism among Europeans. While there is a direct connection in how environmental influences and the human mind helps to understand the nature of racism, it also suggests that Europeans had no control over their environment, which could account for behavioral differences in contemporary Europeans.

Now, that's not to say critics will not take issue with this theory. Some critics will accuse theorists of ignoring the role of perception in racism. Nevertheless, it does not ignore any aspect of perception. It actually takes into account the understanding that Europeans are caught in the middle of evolution. Early Europeans bonded their genes or ad-mixed with several variations of human species, which ensured their survivability. As a result, today's researchers say Europeans are not pure Homo sapiens. Therefore, any contemporary changes in perception can be attributed to evolutionary processes, ceteris paribus.

Another issue among critics will be the amount of concern with change and situational influences on racism. Remember, perception is preset by the transmission of genetic and epigenetic information between generations to ensure the survival of a species. What I consider to be a small challenge in human endeavor. In fact, Europeans are scheduled to undergo significant changes in evolution over the next 50 thousand years. Therefore, they may be susceptible to change, which may have to do more with the role that environmental experiences play on the enduring qualities of human beings. In other words, if Europeans refused to adapt to their current situation, then evolution may change their perceptual outlook on life.

The theory also takes into account the role biology plays in racism. But, it does not negate the role evolution continues to play in human development, which means I try to explain the complex nature of racism in the European through a multitude of scientific lenses. Considerably, I, like Carl Rogers, believe there are certain influences at work which prevent people, perhaps entire populations, from reaching their full potential as human beings.

For example, White supremacy results from environmental experiences and situational influences which, until recently, Europeans had little to no control over. In this case, there may be a few critics who believe humans are the masters of their fate and the captains of their souls. However, their criticism will not consider the natural limitations of humanity. That is to say, humans are worldly creatures, mundane even. However, we have a long way to go before becoming heavenly.

Certain constraints continue to prevent Europeans from taking control of their destiny. The result is they continue to carry the dark cloud of conflict. In many cases, they would rather distort and devalue their sense of humanity rather than mirror what others want them to be. In this regard, Europeans are stubbornly resistant to change. Here, I share an intriguing perspective on racism, which gives special insight on the European mindset. Unconditional positive regard, empathy, and genuineness are Carl Rogers' terms for understanding enduring human qualities necessary to establish healthy intergroup relations. You can use the techniques found in this contemporary theory to change people's perspectives about themselves so they can learn to get along better with others.

A Contemporary Perspective
on Emotional Detachment
Theory

The relationships of power between Whites and Blacks are driving or energizing forces which involve both the process of social and psychological change. It is well within our capacity to change our perception of ourselves and our world. In this perspective, Europeans are stubbornly resistant to change.

My Personal Approach

I've done my homework! In this perspective on racism, I looked at the symbolic meaning of humanity and the deep inner workings of the racist mind. I also believe that nature and nurture play a considerable role in the development of racism. So, I emphasize that environmental experiences and situational influence help determine the nature of racism. I need you to understand that this multifaceted approach to understanding racism is not limited to new perspectives.

Like some of the most admired researchers of my day, I began my inquiry into understanding racism by observing those who were troubled. Understanding this knotty problem, I examined a world that prevented people from having healthy intergroup relations and reaching their full potential as human beings.

Emotional Detachment Theory

I believe that Europeans emotionally detached themselves from their own humanity through prehistoric sources of aggression. We have an inborn connection that serves as an emotional or spiritual link between the mind and body, something White supremacy alienates its members from in order to harness power to dehumanize Black people. Since Europeans lost that profound emotional or spiritual connection to their own humanity, they lost the ability to identify with and understand the Black struggle, their feelings and difficulties.

For example, Europeans love to witness soulful expressions of music and dance, but hate when they cannot feel or experience a spiritual connection to it. Therefore, they resent Black people so much they steal and appropriate soulful or spiritual connections from other cultures to compensate for it. It is disheartening to learn that Europeans are so spiritually disconnected from the mind and body that they need the eternal flame to light their soul in order to reconnect to their humanity.

Curiously, this cognitive disconnection between the mind, body, and spirit (soul) allows them to remain consistent in their own beliefs or actions. Such consistency, done deliberately, especially with the goal of promoting rapid progress, allows for the exploitation, oppression, and humiliation of Black people. However, there are con-sequences for losing their sense of humanity. For example, Europeans become bound by the physical rather than the spiritual world. And they lose their understanding of the universe's plan for humanity in which the answer to who we are as a whole lie among the cosmos.

In the tradition of Carl Rogers, I believe that the challenge is in helping the European race achieve more empathy and positive regard for others. Unconditional positive regard raises confidence in one's self-concept or self-image. There are many ways Europeans can learn to achieve empathy. For example, you might hear a Black person tell a White person, "I don't like your attitude or your behavior. But, I value you and care about you as a person." In other words, kill them with kindness. Each one of us has the ability to connect to others and raise their level of compassion for themselves and the world.

While empathy is crucial to helping others understand themselves and the surrounding world, being genuine is every bit as crucial. Being genuine means opening up your feelings and removing the pretenses and personas. Each of these conditions—positive regard, empathy, and genuineness—are necessary for conducting healthy intergroup relations. In the end, when you attribute your feelings to a person, your compassion will continue to spread throughout the community more profound than its initial impact. In essence, the ripple effect of "Each one teaches one" becomes a vast sea of knowledge, learning, and experiences.

Racism is a manifestation of power and domination of one race over another. The elimination of such victimization—that is to say, exploitation, oppression, or humiliation—requires the development of human society in a way that is compatible with the needs of Blacks, providing them with equal opportunities to develop lifestyles in a social climate free of racism. Given the increasing incidences of hate crimes and other incidences of victimization, it's crucial that everyone understands the nature of racism.

In chapter 7, we will have a serious discussion on how the European will to conquer leads to the violence of intellectual paroxysm. It is a deep discussion on how White society has turned their internal problems against our most vulnerable.

149 | Page

CHAPTER 7
The Violence of Intellectual Paroxysm

…I knew that I could never again raise my voice against the violence of the oppressed in the ghettos without having first spoken clearly to the greatest purveyor of violence in the world today—my own government.

Martin Luther King, Jr. (1953 – 1968)

Dr. King realized that Black aggression was the result of being subjected to harsh or cruel forms of domination. It was only when the government showed its true nature that he understood that Whites displaced their aggression onto Blacks to justify their barbarism. Dr. King knew his response to the amount of violence that Blacks endured at the government's expense would draw backlash. But, he understood the need to bring balance to a society on the verge of moral catastrophe.

Once in awhile, I'll ask the question, "Which is harder? For a barbarian to act civilized or for a civilized person to act like a barbarian? The answer to that question is, "It is harder for a barbarian to act like a civilized person." Most people failed to understand the reason why. Barbarians are unrestrained and not bound by the rule of law as they live freely in nature. Barbarians would not be taught to share or socially interact with people outside of their immediate environment. And when severely provoked, they would not have the presence of mind to endure or, perhaps, resolve conflict issues. In fact, it's more likely that they would retaliate with unrestrained violence.

In contrast, civilized people are taught to show admirable restraint even when physically provoked to retaliate. Many civilized people are enlightened and sophisticated through exposure to intellectual activities necessary for the establishment of healthy intergroup relations. In fact, they've been taught to endure. Yet, they understand when to bear hardship to create lasting peace. Barbarians are thought to have no such understanding as they live life on a day-to-day basis.

This analogy, though a bit long winded, was used to help show the relationships of power between Whites and Blacks. Blacks do not have the presence of mind to express intergroup violence, especially when recurrent. Their humanity prevents them from doing so, even in retaliation for the atrocities committed against them by Whites. Granted, Blacks are thought to be uncivilized. Yet, the greatest amount of violence comes from White aggression.

There is a common theme among Whites today. They believe that the Black man will not seek gainful employment. Therefore, he cannot adequately provide for his family in their time of need. More importantly, he is said to be violent, shiftless, and lazy. Yes, Black men are said to be all those things. But, what Whites have shown the world is more appalling than what we know to be true of any race.

The aforementioned does nothing to strengthen the character of Blacks. Yet, given ordinary conditions, Blacks are a rather peaceful and productive people. They always have been.

Ironically, Blacks are taught to think of Whites as wholesome or good-natured people. In this way, they are systematically desensitized to the violence of intellectual paroxysm expressed by Whites. For example, Blacks are taught to believe Whites saved Black people from themselves by civilizing their African ancestors. Blacks are further taught to think of US slavery as an unfortunate consequence of the civilization process. That had not Whites responded, aggressively, to the situation in Africa, Blacks would have destroyed their selves.

Curiously, religion reinforces their humanity to show kindness or compassion for Whites and others. In contrast, the abuse displayed by White police officers when the circumstance does not call for such violence creates conflict issues in ways that Black tolerance should quickly diminish. Yet, they continue to show more accepting attitudes toward Whites than in the past two or three decades.

Simply because it's justified on network media, Blacks believe they are racially inferior. Television creates the willingness to believe such lies. Radio, magazines, and newspapers reinforce the idea as a fact or realization of life. And human society teaches Blacks how to come to terms with it all. For example, laws are set forth to govern contemporary attitudes in the Black community. It wasn't until social integration that many of these laws were enacted. Law enforcement was reassigned to enforce obedience of law instead of increasing protection from theft of property. For that very reason, some Blacks tolerate the presence of White authority without protest.

Internal Conflict's Influence
on White People's Attitude
Toward Black People

John Locke once said, "The actions of men are the best interpreters of their thoughts." Does the act of doing change your belief system? If you engage in a hate crime, will you have more of a negative attitude toward people who remind you of your pass transgressions? If you reform from racism, are you more likely to extol the benefits of developing positive relationships with people you once opposed?

Law enforcement has become extremely aggressive or violent due to its reassignment. In fact, we are living in a day and age where the murder of young Black males by White police is a recurring event. We have more than two million people imprisoned in this country, most of whom are overwhelmingly Black. Blacks are the most incarcerated people on the planet with mass incarceration rates increasing for young Black women.

Over the past two decades, we've had an unprecedented loss of Black lives followed by a gross increase in prison incarceration for the younger generation of Blacks. We also have major crises happening in various realms of American society. Education, health care, and public housing have many Blacks at-risk. In fact, America is at war against Black people. Thus, we've come to the moment when people must take action to avoid utter and complete disaster or else the country will destabilize.

The sudden or intense outburst of violence displayed by White police spark conflict and hatred between Whites and Blacks. You would think that Black tolerance for White aggression would diminish considerably. But, I'm confused as to whether today's Blacks are in a state of psychological conflict or anxiety. Or, is it their humanity keeping them from retaliating against their oppressors. The resulting matter appears to be a contradiction between simultaneously held beliefs, which causes Blacks to develop attitude problems.

We are at a state of national crisis right now. Chronic life conditions create psychological conflict for Blacks today. Psychological conflict creates personal threats to young Blacks and their existence. It causes confusion and uncertainty to be exact. Increased conflict and tensions create highly stressful periods where there can be no resolution to end a crisis. The period of crisis often involves increased homicide, suicide, family abuse, and substance abuse for many acculturating people who are simply trying to become successful in their lives or careers. Such crises threaten the existence of young Blacks. And while Blacks are oblivious to the declaration of intent, Whites are carrying out their threat to harm or endanger the lives of unsuspecting Blacks. Fatal shootings or the deliberate murders of 12-year-old Tamir Rice and 20-year-old Daunte Wright are among the many ways the system is already destabilizing.

We definitely have a problem in this country when the younger generation of Blacks becomes more vulnerable than the disabled. We definitely have a problem.

One can imagine that the sudden onset or intensification of violence will stigmatize Whites, especially the recurrent abuse of Blacks from White police officers. Yet, it is Blacks who are labeled as socially unacceptable or undesirable. There is no shame or disgrace attached to police abuse or White violence in this country. No sir, there isn't! Their behavior is state-sanctioned thus there are no penalties imposed for murdering Black people. To deliberately harm someone without provocation or call for harm is not only antithetical, it is a dualistic conflict between spirituality and materialism. So, one might ask how did Whites come to gain such an advantage? Whites (Europeans) took a dark and menacing path to reaching enlightenment. They created an intellectual movement that emphasized science and logic greatly at the expense of spiritual understanding. The result is they lost much of their ability to perceive themselves as, well quite frankly, members of the human race.

Their bout began with the desire to control or rule a world they felt left them behind, repeated through endless conquest as acquired by force of arms and under a false appearance of friendship, allied ship, educator, leader, and the false banner of religious faith. They struggled over the spiritual and material nature of Christian worship. The church struggled to resolve the philosophies and knowledge of Gnosticism. Christians went to war with the Arabs. Science and religion have always been in conflict. The Catholics waged war against the Protestants. The European world fought the Nazis. European nations fought over the concept of race. And it looks as if we are about to head into another cold war with communist Russia.

White history is saturated with violence over spiritual and material conflicts. Such psychopathology is symptomatic of their social inadequacies. And their social inadequacies make them believe the world must be divided in order for Whites to fit in. In this way, Whites will achieve freedom for the individual but at a loss of knowledge of self and belonging to this world. The negative feelings acquired by Whites are symptomatic of alienation and identity loss so much so that Whites felt compelled to reinvent history. And it doesn't stop there. The loss of cultural and psychological contact with humanity is so disheartening for them that Whites created their own continent and called it Europe. That's right, Europe is not a continent. It is a peninsula off the continent of Asia. Truly with no place to call home, the mindset of Whites has been full of violent emotions and uncontrollable agitation. As a result, their race has been busy rewriting the pages of world history.

As puzzling as it seems to be, Whites have made attempts to justify their aggression. They not only normalize it in the pages of history rewritten by scholars like Aristotle, Plato, and Socrates, it's reinforced through the social context of politics where history was further distorted by America's founding fathers. John Hancock, George Washington, Benjamin Franklin, and other members of the convention who drafted the US Constitution justified White aggression as necessary to achieve a high level of cultural and social organization in human society.

They said it was absolutely necessary to know when they should bear hardship to create lasting peace. There are scholars today who also say that over the years, since Whites modernized Western civilization, they have taught the world to behave in more socially and culturally acceptable ways. They use liberal changes in conservative lifestyles between the Taliban men and Afghan women as a prime example. Precisely since nonwhites are bemused by White arrogance, as they have been proudly contemptuous, there has been new effort to make sense out of their seemingly senseless behavior.

There have been countless wars waged against the world in the name of peace. And, Whites have had more than their fair share of it. The US Civil War, the Boer War, the First World War, and the Russian Civil War are among the many periods of hostility between Western and Northern countries that set Whites apart from other races. As senseless as many of these wars were, their peculiar obsession with conquering shows White aggression to be unusual or unexpected compared to the aggression found among other races. It is the violence of intellectual paroxysm that motivates the European will to conquer. No other wars or conflicts made by nonwhites on the grounds of tyranny or peace measures up to the kind of violence that makes White aggression appear so senseless. Clashes between the Romans and barbarians, the Greeks and the Egyptians, the fall of Kemet, and the many wars between and among European nations, were so frequent and senseless that it continues to perplex the most aggressive supporters of war.

In a similar vein, whenever a developing country or racial group displays the same level of aggression, understand that they have adopted a Western mentality. And as we have seen through past actions, nothing inherently good will come from it. White aggression is so extreme that it prevents their people from coping with conflicts issues that exist among their own race. They absolutely have no tolerance for dissension from other races. That would be absurd!

Other races have learned to tolerate or cope with dissension as a matter of choice. Thus, it's the ability of the White race to produce extreme levels of violence that makes their intellectual history appear absurd to other races. It's a bit of a paradox; but, is there any real reason why their behavior could be justified? Now, this doesn't mean Whites are inherently bad people. But, they have yet to show the qualities characteristic of humanity. At best, Whites are a rough and tumble people greatly misunder-stood. At worst, they are a sadistic people absolutely determined to conquer the world, regardless of how previously innocent most people were to them. Whatever the case may be, countries are mimicking Western behavior in a desperate attempt to keep pace with the White race.

For the rest of humanity, there is no place in history where Western ideology is justified. Thus, there is no way to explain the overuse of aggression as being well-founded. White aggression is an unprovoked attack on humanity. It results from internal conflicts occurring within the White race. Then they project their intellectual problems onto nonwhites to justify White aggression. In this way, nonwhites will develop feelings of social inadequacy and begin to think of themselves as being problematic even though they do not share in White adversities. And what adversities do Whites share?

Whites share in internal conflict. Thus, they need to overcome their internal struggles. For some odd reason, their struggles have always manifested from a superiority complex. It seems like after learning most of the world had already been conquered or, at least, colonized, the realization of it all would have stifled their ambitions. But, this complex has a peculiar hold on their race. Thus, they simply dominate those who already won by conquest, making Whites the greatest conquerors of all.

How odd is it that the White race continues to profess their superiority even after they were forced to whitewash history to hide their truth? Their motivation appears to come from being overly aggressive which, in their eyes, made them better than nonwhites. Such a complex runs deep within the White race. Perhaps, it's the exaggerated aggression that drives their will to conquer. After all the success and failures of conquest, one could only wonder if the negative feelings of losing are masked with bouts of supremacy. Or, could it be the duality of intellectual conflicts that drives their will to dominate others. Either way, it appears that the world has adopted their complex. Yet, most people do not have the mindset to adapt that level of aggression.

What Distinguishes
Humans from other
Species

According to some scholars, what makes human beings stand out from other species is their ability to effectively use spoken or written words as a communication system. It appears that humans are the only species that can communicate their behavior, thoughts, and feelings in both spoken and written words. No other species have the ability. Other species communicate their thoughts and feelings through behavior and sound. They do not communicate through spoken or written word systems.

Human's ability to communicate their behavior, thoughts, and feelings through spoken or written communication is what sets them apart from other species. This revelation permitted new forms of communications. First, humans had to evolve their communication into a more complex or advanced language system. They accomplished this feat by learning to create spoken or written language.

It would take quite a few evolutionary cycles just to conceive of such a notion. From earlier forms of communication, humans realized that signs, shapes, and symbols could be used to create a better system of communication. This opened the door for signs to be used as a language system. There was some universal truth to signing. Along with using shapes and symbols, sign language took on its own set of conventions. Thus, communication took on distinct social meaning.

It wasn't too long afterwards humans realized they could communicate through signs, shapes, and symbols, they categorized various aspect of it and gave it names like the Latin alphabet, ALSO referred to as the Roman alphabet, now English alphabet. It would take centuries for it to develop into a proper language system, the letter "J" being the last letter of the English alphabet to be added. From the development of various language systems, they realized communication could be preserved and expressed through spoken or written language systems even though it would be very complex.

For example, there are four principles of language within the English language system: grammar, vocabulary, phonology, and discourse. Each system revolves around the English alphabet. There are two main ways in which we can communicate the English alphabet. The first is directly through the use of the English alphabet. And the other is through a set of symbols we call Braille. There are no other animals on the planet that can be taught to communicate through the use of these systems. Although apes and gorillas can communicate up to eight hundred signs through sign language, it should not be mistaken for an alphabet system but a behavioral form of communication.

We even learned to expand our use of communication by studying the relationships among signs, shapes, and symbols. Arithmetic, algebra, geometry, trigonometry, and calculus helped us to think of communication in an entirely new spectrum. Mathematics was the scientific tools of discovery that taught humans how to think in broader cultural dimensions. Sometime thereafter, humans learned that whosoever controlled spoken or written language could rewrite history.

We talked earlier about Whites being concerned with recording history. Their objective is to cover-up facts about the dark path they took to achieve enlightenment. We've already mentioned the sixty-five-thousand-year history they spent trapped between fire and ice. We've also covered the daunting reality that Whites only recently evolved. Therefore, they have no historical claims that would place them among the experiences and accomplishments of Africans without first acknowledging Black people. So, they carry the dark cloud of conflict. In this way, Whites are obsessed with achieving supremacy. They also believe that there are consequences for their actions in the near future if ever they were to relax and stop discriminating against nonwhites, especially if they change their contemporary attitudes toward Black people.

From current times to the very near past, Whites have shown themselves to be extremely dangerous. Chattel slavery, two periods of eugenics, one under slavery and the other under the banner of scientific racism, segregation, prejudice, and discrimination well into the new millennium, Whites have raped, pillaged, and plundered virtually every race on the planet. In fact, their violent response to Blacks come from having continuous conflict issues between simultaneous but incompatible desires, needs, drives, or impulses. In this way, their mental struggles are said to be the very reason why Whites perceive human races to be separate and distinct.

Language has been the White man's tool to persuade people to change their perceptual outlook on life. Ever since they learned how to manipulate it, Whites have been tooling along the planet, conquering at a staggering pace. Today, Whites have definitely put distance between themselves and nonwhites as they strive to make progress in this competitive environment call Western civilization.

Whites realize that through communication they can control every aspect of modern life, including their own, which will prove they are the greatest conquerors of humanity. Most countries prefer to tell history from their perspectives. It allows them to hide the most unfortunate aspects of their past. It also enables people to present themselves ways that are false but personally advantageous. And for the White race, the ultimate goal has always been to be supreme rulers of the universe. To control the narrative or influence the thinking strategies of world cultures, the planet, even control the moon along its very ecliptic, is the will of the European.

For Whites, conquering is not seen as a dehumanizing and ultimately futile activity. It simply marks a significant transition in human evolution. Along with the right to freewill, they believe it is human nature to choose or control their own destiny. Controlling the narrative is an ingenious or devious way to persuade people to follow Whites opposed to conquering them through brutality. In their minds, controlling the narrative, even whitewashing history, is considered to be a peaceful or more evolved way of conquering. Although, as Whites approach the halfway mark in twenty-first century politics, more are saying they'd like to get out of this rat race and retire to an isolated retreat away from the hassles of Western civilization.

There are certain secrets in life Europeans would prefer not to bring to the light of day. One of these secrets is that the concept of race is nothing more than a rat race or a fight to achieve, not only success but, supremacy before others can achieve it. What a complex, right? If you think I'm wrong, an important part of their intellectual history is their obsession with controlling the narrative and/or whitewashing history. Their obsession with partaking in the European vacation, their obvious obsession with understanding religion and communicating with the supernatural, their obsession with westernizing developing countries, and their obsession with conquering entire nations, all speaks to the will of Europeans. Their exaggerated or obsessive feelings about being better than others consume their race with particular force. Such a complex is thought to have been a behavior of early modern Europeans, a people thought to be extinct.

This book, Against Black People: The European Will to Conquer, hints at the notion that today's Whites continue to exist as Cro-Magnon or early modern Europeans. They say the only difference between Homo sapiens and the Cro-Magnon is the level of aggression. We do know that the only people on this planet who are true Homo sapien or Homo sapien sapien are Africans. All other people on the planet are thought to be adulterated with other racial mixtures.

Cro-Magnon, the earliest known form of modern Europeans, is thought to be highly aggressive by nature.

But since aggression is more of an environmental experience, I would contend that the intellectual development of the Cro-Magnon enabled him to rationalize his unique position on survival. Survival of the fittest and kill or be killed: It is easy to understand why so many people misuse both terms. Having the ability to reason or the right to freewill enables Whites to act in ways that is beyond human conception.

Again, I am not saying that White people are inherently bad. But, they've come to be a serious problem in human society. Their proven violence and sense of entitlement comes from their direct obsession with wanting to rule the universe. Their desire to rule above all others does nothing to show kindness or compassion for the rest of humanity. The goal of humanity is for humans to exist in ways we would consider to be characteristic of human beings as a whole. The fact that Whites continues to transgress threatens the very nature of humanity.

In theory, the Ice Age changed the will of early Europeans. They endured great violence and brutality during that prolonged period. The level of violence and brutality that exists within the modern-day European is reminiscent of that time.

Today, there may very well be remnants of Cro-Magnon behavior found among modern-day Europeans (Whites, if you will). If they fail to curve their behavior (fail to overcome that very thing that makes them aggressive) and continue to resist change in fear of being adversely affected—much like in their fear of racial and cultural diversity—then evolution just may pass them by.

And if evolution passes over the White race, then they may go extinct much like the Neanderthal.

Remember, the Neanderthal was maladaptive thus incapable of change. In fact, they eventually died out due to their inability to adapt to changes in the social environment. More accurately, they were absorbed by Cro-Magnon more so than becoming extinct. We find evidence of Neanderthal DNA existing in modern-day Europeans, about five to seven percent of it to be accurate. And thanks to the raping, pillaging, and plundering of vast civilizations, we can find traces of it around the globe.

In this chapter, among others, we have seen that violence factors into our understanding of the human condition. It is an important determinant of human behavior. Racism, sexism, and aggression give special insight into the nature of humans and provides context for the way we are perceived by others in the world around us. In addition, violence is involved in the natural selection process of human evolution. We've read about a few aspects of violence and human evolution so far in this book. The fact that violence continues to exist among humans shows us it is an important factor of natural selection. In the next chapter, we will turn our attention to the fascinating world of Whites and their motivation behind the concept of race.

CHAPTER 8
The Concept of Race

McGuire, 2022

Oh, I maintain that race is the phoniest issue ever invented by the mind of man. The European invented and developed the concept of race. Really, there is no such thing as race because nature created no races. Race is a manmade thing… If you go back and look at an old dictionary, you won't even find a definition for a race. Race grew out of the pseudoscientific development of Europe…

John Henrik Clarke (1973)

I have no idea how many times I've heard people say race is a social construct. Leading scholars say it was invented by Europeans who wanted the world to believe Whites were separate and distinct from the rest of humanity. They also say the term race was used to justify their proposed superiority over nonwhites.

People like Jane Elliott say we are all part of one race, the human race. We know this because archeologist Joe Hanson found our oldest ancestor, Dinkinesh. Sometimes referred to as Lucy, she is approximately three and a half million years old. We also know that Africa created the complete man or the first modern man about two hundred thousand years ago, a number that continues to be pushed back. What was also established by a researcher named Rebecca Cann is that all human organisms can be traced to an African woman who lived about two hundred thousand years ago. She has the DNA of humanity in her genetic makeup. In fact, the mitochondrial Eve gene can be traced to a group of women who are still living in Africa. So, they have the genes necessary to produce children of every race (hue) in their DNA. No other beings on the planet have that genetic sequence (ability) in their

DNA. Also, what we recently discovered is our internal organs are anatomically African, regardless of racial origin.

On that note, the Supreme Court says race is a biological construct. I am inclined to agree with them. But, what do I know. I'm neither a teacher nor a sociologist. I'm not a geneticist or a biologist. I've already said that while Whites introduced the concept of race to justify their place in the world, I believe it is very much a natural progression of evolution.

I do believe we all come from the same race, the human race. However, humans evolved into separate and distinct races over the course of evolution. Curiously, the idea that, over the course of evolution, people moved away from the equator, creating distinct visible characteristics between them, does little to satisfy my intellect. I do understand the theory, though. It goes on to say that those who moved furthest away from the equator changed in primary physical characteristics. Europeans moved furthest away from the equator. Thus, they underwent the greatest physiological changes. These physical variations in visible characteristics resulted from the interaction between their genetic makeup and the environment; and in the minds of Europeans, that justified them using the term white to characterize their people, White meaning free from genetic impurities.

So far, there's no real problem with that theory. I can honestly say, "We're all in agreement here." But where we differ is in the evolutionary process of change. People often negate the fact that evolution changes organisms over time. And like any organism, humans must adapt and respond to change. Europeans (i.e., the White race), for example, was isolated from the outside world for an extended period of time. In theory, evolution should have left them behind. But, it didn't. They changed!

Much like in Charles Darwin's book, The Descent of Man, Europeans started out from the same biological systems (i.e., Blacks or Africans in theory), and then adapted and responded to changes in the environment. One of these changes controlled or influenced sexual selection.

In sexual selection, a female chooses to mate with a male whose traits she determines to be most beneficial for breeding. This event ensures her offspring will develop into healthy and fully functioning people, hence survival of the fittest. Try to remember that the Grimaldis, who were African at the time, were the first modern humans to populate prehistoric Europe. Some say, they ad-mixed with the Neanderthal. Others say the Grimaldis adopted a genetic strand called the SLC245 gene. Along with ad-mixing, it did create a separate and distinct breed of humans, just not a new species. Europeans evolved enough in their physical characteristics that appearance influenced their breeding selection. These visible (physical) characteristics created variations not only among the Neanderthal and other European primates, but among the Grimaldis. Fast forward to modern times and the same natural laws apply to modern-day humans.

On a similar note of importance, it is well within the nature of humans to adapt and respond to changes in the environment. Thanks to epigenetics, we now understand that psychological (intrapsychic) trauma can change the thought processes of humans, completely, and in one generation. Trauma can also change the human thought process without involving changes to DNA sequences.

As you can see, it's the concept of race I reflect on in this chapter. Changes in social forces raise questions that are extremely important to the future of humanity. This chapter can help answer challenging questions that lie ahead by turning up the unexpected. Before we end our book discussion on Against Black People: the European Will to Conquer, we need to know more about the concept of race. I find it necessary to help explain its complex nature in order to gain a better understanding of the human condition.

Understanding Race and Ethnicity

This chapter may sound familiar to many of you. That's because I addressed similar topics in earlier chapters. So then, why rehash it? Well, I would like to regard it in a different way. I find it necessary to give careful consideration to all details and aspects of the word race in order for you to gain better insight on the human condition.

It is my intention to prove that regardless of its construct, there is much more to the word race. While critics see it as little more than a justification to discriminate against Black people under the banner of research, using its social construction is an excuse for ignoring the entire concept. Ignoring the concept of race frees White people from blame or criticism for their violent and barbaric behavior shown over the centuries.

There are many ways in which Europeans discriminate against Black people. They use racial distinction as the primary way to discriminate. Although they are supposed to be a fair-minded lot of people, Europeans use racial distinction to further their own biases. Some even claim that certain races have a biological inherence that gives them an adaptive advantage over other races. Thus, in keeping with the theme in this book, let's look at race and see how it has taken on distinct social meanings.

Race was first introduced as a biological concept. It was used to distinguish between breeds of plants and animals: tall, short, long, small, stocky build, et cetera. These distinctions among various groups of organisms later served to justify the color schemes of humans: White, Black, Brown, and the like. Today, race refers to a group of humans who are readily identified by the same physical characteristics such as skin color. Hence, race is one of the most misused and misunderstood words in the English language system. Loosely, it has taken on various social meanings. Everything from a person's religion to their ethnic identity has been used to determine one's race.

There are three main racial categories used to classify the human race. Asiatic or Asian, Caucasoid, European or sometimes White, and Africoid, African or, generally speaking, Black is used to clarify differences among distinct groups of people. Skin color, hair texture, facial features, and other primary physical characteristics are the most widely use markers to determine race. However, thanks to ad-mixing, these racial classifications are losing its usefulness.

Today, many people define race as a social construct. Why? It is based on the perception of people who accept as fact certain myths and stereotypes about others who physically differ from them. For example, some people continue to believe that Asians are naturally industrial, Jews are inherently greedy, and Hispanics are simply lazy. What people choose to believe about others have profound social consequences on the human mind. Not so long ago, for example, Blacks were denied access to schools, hospitals, churches, and other institutions based on skin color.

There are even scholars who claim that biological differences make one group of people more adaptive than another. They believe that biological inherence is the reason why Whites are so adaptive thus superior to other races. Some scholars even believe humans are a separate and distinct species from one another. Also in America, where pseudoscience and slavery forged a grim alliance, Whites attributed to Blacks any characteristics that made it necessary to enslave them in captivity, indefinitely.

Unfortunately, racism still has a stranglehold on race research. While some scholars and researchers have given up on their research arguments, others argue that evolution created racial differences among various groups of people. They believe that certain differences can be seen in sexual behavior, intelligence, and in criminality. Most of these traits were explained in a book called The Bell Curve, a reference book published by Richard Herrnstein and Charles Murray in 1994.

In the book, Herrnstein and Murray explain variations in human intelligence within American society. The authors created a theory that, according to critics, is filled with vulgar remarks and stereotypes. Their book is filled with information most people frequently misinterpret and oversimplify in order to get them onboard and in agreement with their racially prejudicial views. Sadly, even misused or misinterpreted theories like the one presented by Herrnstein and Murray can be of use to us. Although people who use The Bell Curve often develop their own theories, they do so with the further hope of justifying racism.

Although the basis of race is indeed biological, its interpretations allow it to exist as a sociological construct. Now is a good time to tell you it is ethnicity we think about when discussing the topic of race. Religion, language, heritage, and group behavior make up one's ethnicity. Race has absolutely nothing to do with ethnicity. Although ethnicity is often mistaken for race, it is not. For example, Jews are not a race. They are part of a religious denomination. Therefore, people from any race can practice Judaism. Considering that religion is an institution born from social customs and cultural traditions, it stands to reason that Jews constitute an ethnic group, not a racial group.

Caryn Elaine Johnson, professionally known as Whoopi Goldberg, is currently a television personality on the hit TV talk show "The View." She was removed from the show and temporarily suspended for making what people felt was an extreme accusation. Whoopi stated that the Jewish Holocaust was not about race. That it is about man's inhumanity toward man. Judaism is not a race. To her accreditation, the Jews who suffered through the Holocaust were European, White if you will. Whites adopted Judaism as their religion in early Europe. However, they do not descend from nor are they born from the blood of Abraham. Therefore, they are not Jew by race but by religious denomination.

The Zionist Jews (Whites) who largely populate Israel today have adopted the belief that their religious status as Jew constitutes a separate and distinct race, which is simply not true. Again, it is a religious denomination. A large portion of the Jewish population is European or European decent. Only a small minority are of the original inhabitants descend from bloodline. In a similar vein, Nick Cannon, earned himself a one-year suspension for permitting Professor Grief (who was a member of the legendary Rap group Public Enemy) to speak on the Zionist's agenda in America. Nick's podcast, Cannon's Class: Class is Now in Session, is an educational program that brings Black topics to the cultural mainstream.

After reading this chapter, I hope you will learn to understand the differences between race and ethnicity. For sure, I've stressed these concepts enough throughout the book. Society does not make such distinctions. As a result, people often talk in racial terms as an important form of social interaction. For example, people often consider what race they would like to associate with when deciding on which state they'd like to live in, which neighborhoods will be more suitable, and which school districts are better equipped to educate their children. Similarly, people tend to use race to determine whether another person is more intelligent, competent, sociable, or socially acceptable. Such thinking is more so learned from parents during early childhood. But, it does not automatically negate the cultural influences of today's society.

Race and the Implication of White Supremacy

While race may not always be about racial prejudice and discrimination, there is a bit of arrogance associated with it. Europeans often behave in a superior or condescending way when interacting with people from other races. Hence, it is important we consider the wider implications of White supremacy.

Europeans behave toward others in ways that show they consider themselves socially or intellectually superior. And, why not! They're the dominant source in the world today. They control much of the world's economy. They also set the tone for mainstream values in politics, fashion, and culture. So why would we not regard European values as preeminent.

Their level of prominence means Europeans exert strong influence over much of the world. However, it's problematic. Their views and high ideals are often taken as the absolute truth. Not many countries question the integrity of Europeans or Whites, either. This passivism makes it hard for independent countries to exert its influence in the world. But, there are a few countries and people working to undo these cultural discrepancies.

The problem is Europeans continue to exert their dominance over the world. Their political tactics work so well, they look good, fair, or just in the eyes of people, causing great concerned for those looking to find and bring an end to their reign. However, there are those who feel like Europeans are showing condescension to people who they feel are less important or intelligent.

The whole idea of Europeans showing dominance in the world began in the fifteenth and sixteenth century, a period of time they call the age of enlightenment. When they rose to power and began to expand throughout the world, Europeans had to justify the slave trade and, as records reflect, the colonial system that followed it. Although modern racism was not a known method of colonizing, it has its roots in British colonial America.

In fact, the very idea of categorizing humans as separate and distinct races was introduced by Carl Linnaeus in 1785. But the word race was introduced to Linnaeus by Georges Louis Buffon. Buffon introduced it into the scientific community in 1749. He generalized his used of the word to mean kind or variety. Buffon also found out that he could breed new strains of plants and animals from genetically different hosts. And much like when a tiger and lion are mated, the offspring (a liger) is infertile. So, Buffon defined a species as a group of organisms that could reproduce fertile offspring. Carl Linnaeus may have borrowed the concept of race from Buffon. But, as we already know, Johann Friedrich Blumenbach (1775) grouped humans into six racial categories, five of which he used to explain the presence of humans living in America at the time.

Blumenbach based his entire premise on the notion that race could be adapted as a biological marker to measure intellect, achievement, or ability. But, he failed to attach significant biological definitions to it. Perhaps, understanding that Europeans and Africans were of the same race (the human race) would discourage Europeans from enslaving them. How can you enslave a humane people who were the creators of Western civilization and Christian religion? Would they not exist as an extension of you? In fact, you would have to acknowledge their contributions to world as a whole.

In order to justify their enslavement, people like Blumenbach continued to dehumanize them. They stripped Africans of their humanity. Still, his efforts would serve as the foundation for certain humans on the planet to be classified as slaves.

Dually noted, there was no way humanly possible for any Africans who were enslaved to be the same people who stepped off of the boat in North America and the Caribbean islands. The amount of psychological trauma endured during middle passage changed who they were as a people. But, I digress!

Curiously, the word race was originally discussed in the abstract and had no implications or suggestions of social meaning. It was simply an observation meant to be used to help explain the nature of relationships among plants and animals (e.g., humans). That despite obvious physical characteristics associated with evolving in various geographical regions, all humans were of the same species.

Its Proven Use: The
Concept of Race

Although Blumenbach used the word race with the intention to cause harm, it has proven to be useful. It helps the individual person to group people into human categories until he or she can fully process new information about them. We often group people into racial categories when new information is too much to process at one time. Overtime, we learn to consider new information by first recognizing or acknowledging what is familiar to us then considering the rest as we go.

Grouping people into racial categories is a natural process. For the individual person, it is a way for him or her to figure out whether strangers are good people. In this way, they can decide for themselves whether a stranger is worthy of their consideration. In many of today's cases, when we categorize people, new scenarios involve fear of race, ethnic, sex, age, religion, nationality, or other notable characteristic differences. Regardless of the official or outward declaration, grouping people gives the individual person a right to maintain control over his or her own existence when deciding the nature of new relationships. The problem is people often come into immediate conflict with strangers when they make stark judgments about them. They also create conflict problems and racial tension when they generalize about strangers in ways that do not consider any variation from one person to the next. In this case, what's happening here is rather personal.

Most times, holding a personal grudge against a total stranger has to do with unresolved problems that might stem from early childhood trauma. In this case, a person might fail to see possible similarities between himself or herself and the group to which the individual belongs. Or, the person who is racist may fail to understand they share in common such things as interests, beliefs, or political goals. In this case, they believe that each race has qualities and abilities that are inherently different thus some races are superior and others inferior. Therefore, the very idea of socially interacting with strangers becomes offensive to them.

This is perhaps what Gordon W. Allport meant when he said prejudice can be extinguished over time through the use of education or information. However, what he failed to consider, in the case of racist people, was their beliefs or opinions progressed beyond the limitations set by the nature of prejudice.

Racism is a syndrome of hate. It can be viewed as any type of prejudice or discrimination that is backed by institutional power. Ageism, sexism and, as I said before, conservatism are among the many degrees, secessions, and aggressions we characterize as racism. But, how do we identify it? With racism, there is often a group of scenarios or events that form a recognizable pattern that, when occurring together, are indicative of your more pervasive -isms. It is especially true for anyone who finds himself or herself in undesirable situations. All too often, racism involves conflict between two or more competing races or its members.

Racism affects other races. But, it affects the humanity of Whites more than any other race. Why? Their humanity has yet to evolve as a result. Whites have digressed more than any racial group on earth. During the Stone Age, Europeans underwent evolutionary changes that would alter their life-course perspective. Extreme climatic conditions forged their durable nature. Along with ad-mixing with various subspecies, ancient Europeans digress-ed. What you see today are descendants of a nomadic people we call the White race. And they understand their race has yet to fully evolve. Their belief in racial superiority helps them justify their place in the world.

As a nomadic people, Whites pursue personal goals and independence rather than group-oriented goals or interests. We call this concept individualism. Many have self-serving values we might consider to be a bit natural-istic or spontaneous. Sensation-seeking or living for the moment, especially when they place personal interests before other people, shows their impulse to regress to early nomadic states. Conflict, wars, and general aggression, both racial and sexual, show Whites have a strong proclivity for racism.

It's even written in the Declaration of Independence that Whites should follow the pursuit of personal goals and independence rather than taking up collective goals or interests. It was noted when a committee made up of John Adams, Benjamin Franklin, Thomas Jefferson, Roger

Sherman, and Robert Livingston wrote the famous lines that among their unalienable rights, all men shall be endowed with life, liberty, and the pursuit of happiness. It's that level of individualism that sets them apart from the rest of human society.

It is my hypothesis that the White race is Cro-Magnon. Now I know anthropologists say that the Cro-Magnon died out roughly 30 thousand years earlier. But they also say that the only difference between Homo sapiens and Cro-Magnon is the level of violence. Cro-Magnon's violence is forged by the extreme conditions of prehistoric Europe. Curiously, Africans say it is their humanity that prevents them from showing violence toward or against their colonizers. Unfortunately, evidence of the earliest known form of modern Europeans, dating from about 50 thousand to 30 thousand years B.C., points to the development of today's Whites who, admittedly, are still undergoing evolutionary changes. That due to the amount of ad-mixing with various races on the planet, the Cro-Magnon continues to exist as modern-day Whites.

Definitely, Whites are not pure Homo sapiens. In fact, the only pure Homo sapiens on the planet are Africans as so stated in a Yale lecture. As for any evidence that supports the proposition, resources can be found at the Cold Spring Harbor lab in Long Island. We see other, more blatant forms of evidence in the applications of violence found in European (White) behavior.

Applications of Violence

The European will to conquer is rooted in the applications of violence practiced by early nomads or the caveman. Every effort to advance Northern and Western civilizations is a glaring admission of Europeans and their will to conquer the world through racism.

Now, this book is not the first of its caliber. Neither will it be the last to argue this topic. The findings produced in other books often justify racism. Researchers justify their findings by concluding that its impact is followed by some level of progression. Industrialism, modernity, and technological advancement are more often accredited to the progress made through the use of racism. Specifically, White supremacists are recognized for improving the world's economy, science, and medicine. What these researchers fail to inform the public is that racism, even if it does lead to some level of progression, does not benefit the world in its entirety. In effect, its residual impact doesn't matter either. The rapid and widespread practice of racism has had a catastrophic impact on humanity as a whole. Its devastation has fostered an antiblack social climate among Whites, globally.

What differs about this book in comparison to others is the attempt made to underscore important human qualities despite the atrocities created by racism. The shockingly cruel act of racism brought to the world, especially the wanton violence by Whites against Blacks, is a further admission of having a superiority complex that consumes their worldview. The result is the world has been forced to consider life through the aesthetic lens of White male supremacy. This book will provoke quite a few readers to reassess their life-course perspective. In thought, they will come to consider how Europeans have managed to turn so much of the world against Black people.

Who Controls the Narrative?

Throughout their short-lived lives, Europeans (Whites) have been in control of writing history. The problem is, whenever it suits their purpose, they rewrite history to better fit the European narrative. Europeans changed certain historical events to hide unpleasant facts about their past. As I've said before, they continue to hide the truth about the fate of Cro-Magnon who are said to be extinct. Yet, up to now, Europeans have shown many of the same characteristics as the Cro-Magnon. The violent social behavior shown over the centuries toward nonwhites are characteristic patterns of aggression associated with Cro-Magnon man. The total disregard for life outside of the European center is another one of many examples. Also, Whites often hide the European invasion of Northern Africa by Alexander the Great. That story, in and of itself, gives a personal account for the European use of military force in global conquest. For that very reason, they manage to rewrite history in a broader historical context of White supremacy.

We discussed various aspects of European history and more in greater detail throughout this book. However, the point of the research found in this book is to help readers gain a better understanding about the complex nature of Europeans. Europeans were not only the last group of people to evolve in the world but also the last to emerge as world leaders, especially when early civilizations were being developed along the Nile River in Africa and in other parts of the African continent.

I also gave special insight into the psychology of Europeans throughout this book. When Europeans finally established themselves as a nation or group of nations, they came to realize that much of their existence was conditioned on whether they could convince the world they were a separate and distinct race. Being a separate and distinct race of people would hide a profoundly deep complex they had about their place in the world. Hence, they developed the concept of race to help them control the narrative.

We briefly considered these defining moments as we looked into whether Europeans were a separate and distinct race of beings. Much of what we know today about Europeans and the actions they take against Black people are based on empirical research. The findings, arguments, and propositions found in these pages provide important clues. Many of these clues will aid scholars in their battle on important problems associated with racism and White supremacy.

My Reason for Supporting
The Concept of Race

One of the main reasons why I support beliefs like the concept of race is I truly believe it is a part of human evolution. As a part of language, the concept of race has always been around us. We may not have always had the use of spoken or written words but due to the gradual development of human evolution, we evolved to speak and write complex languages. Much like mathematics, language has always been a factor of evolution. And just like mathematics, as the universe continues to expand, more speech groups will evolve, creating infinite language systems.

In brief, it is quite arrogant to assume man created language to sooth his intellect. Language is a natural part of human evolution. Europeans continue to display prideful arrogance or a haughty attitude about the creation of the human language system, often unjustifiably, which influences their thoughts or motives. Both their aggression and the motivation behind it are related to their arrogance and how well they learn to cope with it. Developing the concept of race and using it to control the narrative is one way Whites learned to cope with their superiority complex.

Every chapter in this book is, in a sense, correct. But, there are other ways of looking at European aggression. This book is another avenue for those who'd like to acknowledge or recognize terrible injustices committed against Black people. Now, I'm not saying this book has a better approach for understanding the dark path Europeans have taken to achieve enlightenment. I'm only saying this approach might better serve people for certain purposes. This approach is more useful than accepting the notion that we are all a part of one race, the human race. That approach ignores the atrocities committed by Europeans in the name of White supremacy, something no other race has ever done. Remember, no single approach is right for every situation. This approach serves as an alternative to any approach that's not working.

You will be happy to know that The Concept of Race is the last of this book's 8 chapters. One of the main goals of this book was for you to reflect on its relevance to your own existence. Many unanswered questions about European aggression remain. But, this book does provide important clues about why White people are the why they are; and, why Blacks are treated differently. What could be more important to us all than understanding more about one another? One of the most important themes in life is how to get along with others to make our lives more enjoyable and humane. Following this chapter, you will find an Epilogue that focuses on an aspect of this book I wanted to cover in-depth.

EPILOGUE
The Destruction of Black Civilizations

> It became almost necessary for the European to whiten up a part of Black history when they began to take over the world in the fifteenth and sixteenth century.
>
> John Henrik Clarke (1973)

According to John Henrik Clarke, if we are to believe most White scholarship on Africa is true, then early Africans were primitive savages who could barely use fire. Accordingly, they were crudely simple people who made no contributions to humanity. They didn't build any of the monuments or pyramids found in Africa. Nor did they develop any civilizations worth validating. How could they? They were innately inferior. And if White scholars are correct in their assumptions, then why did we find ourselves gridlocked in a one hundred plus year debate about the destruction of Black civilizations?

Africa was destined for global conflict. Since the very beginnings, resources found in Africa attracted the attention of people from around the world. Africa has been robbed, using violence and often causing damage to its infrastructure, especially while engaged in war with neighboring countries. It's been robbed of its most important resources in the form of human chattel and for its arts and artifacts in which Europeans tried to accredit their ancestors with creating.

Now, the destruction of Black civilizations began with the fall of Africa. Early Africans were highly evolved and profoundly skilled in many occupations. They were skilled in mathematics, writing, sciences, engineering, medicine, religion, the fine arts; and, they built the great pyramids, all of which were African achievements. They were responsible for creating advanced civilizations in every sense of the word. Their achievements were marked by complex social and political organizations, materials, sciences, and artistic progress. What made Africans great was their ability to produce.

Africans produced a large quantity of the world's trade both in goods and services. Their ability to produce commerce on a large scale made them superior merchants with enough surplus goods to effectively compete in international commerce. Africans, the first builders of civilization, frankly, had no idea Europeans, who were still very much undeveloped or uncivilized, could conquer Africa.

Africa, being the cradle of world civilization, fell because it overextended itself. While it was not at-risk of falling into financial ruins, Africa fought excessively against invaders. Africans were not only bombarded by attacks from neighboring countries, but foreign invaders, most with the purpose of acquiring gold, land, and resources. Too much manpower was used, overextending its most precious resources: Men!

The Persians were the first to invade Africa. They invaded Egypt. Historians believe it was Mansa Musa who inspired nations to invade the African continent. The West African King of Mali who, through his generosity, gave away so much gold on his pilgrimage to Mecca, it offset the Egyptian economy for a decade. Word of his wealth quickly spread throughout Middle Eastern Asia. The problem was Egypt sat at the middle of the cross roads into Africa from Asia and Europe. The Persians learned that Africa was a resource hub for gold. So, they used an army and attempted to invade it by force. Europeans would be among the many groups of people to invade Africa, entering from the West.

According to history, it was the Spanish and Portuguese who explored the West African continent for potential conquest. However, they soon realized that taking control of Africa by force of arms was more complex than first considered. The two most important factors were the terrain and people. Africa had a few nations and civilizations. Many of these places had large militaries with fierce warriors commanded by great generals. For Europeans, the one thing Africa was lacking was a source of ignorance. Europeans scoured many terrains in search of places in Africa to conquer. They soon learned that less than a percentage of Africa was tribal or nomadic, which presented itself a problem.

Europeans realized they needed to find a dominant source of weaponry. They scoured the civilized world for dominant weapons, but to no avail. Finally, in China, the Spanish learned of firearms. Firearms were invented in China (1000AD) approximately one hundred years after the Chinese created explosive power (black power or, today, gun power). Their firearms were warehoused after the Chinese decided that type of weaponry was dishonorable. The Chinese were honorable people and for them mass killings were unacceptable. In fact, they consider the use of heavy weaponry (i.e., firearms such as guns, canons, and explosives) morally unacceptable and liable to make citizens lose respect for their emperors. Thus, they decided to stockpile their firearms in warehouses. The Chinese returned to the use of more noble weapons like the trusty sword and loyal spear. Even in many of today's militaries, the sword is carried by military officers as a symbol of nobility. In today's militaries, the spear-tip flag poles used during ceremonial occasions are symbolic of the spear used in early warfare.

What appears to be absent from later history books is the amount of time Span and Portugal needed to prepare for the invasion. Even after adopting the use of firearms, it would take both countries two hundred years to invade Africa. They spent two hundred years planning, strategizing, and militarizing their people for the invasion. The transatlantic slave trade started in 1444, when the Portuguese abducted two hundred thirty-five Africans from the coast of West Africa and auctioned them in Lagos, located in the southern region of Algarve, Portugal.

The British developed English trade and international trade routes to Africa earlier in the process. But, it wasn't until later that Britain would join the Atlantic slave trade and then dominate the industry.

Throughout much of its intellectual history, Africa has not had a fair chance to grow vigorously and healthily. It's the richest continent on the planet in terms of resources and yet we still know nothing about its potential to provide for every nation on earth. We would also like to know why so many Africans had very little chance to be successful and profitable when Africa is so abundant in resources.

The twenty-first century represents an outstanding opportunity for Blacks to learn their history. It is also a good time to gain a better understanding of why so many Whites are against Black people. Blacks need to improve their understanding of who they are as a whole, especially as a people living within a wicked nation. As you can tell from reading chapter 1, it's time for White people to resolve their problems with Blacks so that the world can lay this issue to rest.

Use this book to improve on your understanding of why so many Whites are against Black people. You may even consider dedicating yourself to learning more about the Black experience. That way, you can enlighten the minds of others to the fact that we're all human beings. Surely, the world could use an intervention.

REFERENCES

Africa, Llaila (2022). These people are not like us. Social Media [Online] Available: https://www.youtube.com/watch?v=Ex_xIg1sLs8

Allport, G. (1954). The Nature of Prejudice. Menlo Park, CA: Addison-Wesley.

Alexander, M. (2015). Black Lives Matter. Social Media [Online] Available: https://www.facebook.com/pages/Michelle-Alexander/168304409924191

Alexander, M. (2012). The New Jim Crow: Mass Incarceration in the Age of Colorblindness. New York, NY. The New Press

Berkowitz, L. (1971). The Contagion of Violence: An S-R Mediational Analysis of Some Effects of Observed Aggression. In W. Arnold and M. Page (Eds.), Nebraska Symposium on Motivation (Vol. 18). Lincoln, NE: University of Nebraska Press. (10)

Berkowitz, L. (1983a). Aversively Stimulated Aggression. American Psychology, 38, 1135-1144.(10, 14)

Blascovich, J., Wyer, N.A., Swart, I.A., and Kibler, J.L. (1997). Racism and Racial Categorization. Journal of Personality and Social Psychology, 72, 1364-1372.

Bobo, L. (1988). <u>Group Conflict, Prejudice, and the Paradox of Contemporary Racial Attitudes</u>. In P. A. Katz & D. M. Taylor (Eds.), *Eliminating racism: Profiles in controversy*. New York: Plenum.

Bobo, L. (2000). <u>Race and Beliefs about Affirmative Action: Assessing the Effects of Interests, Group Threat, Ideology, and Racism</u>. In D. O. Sears, J. Sidanius, & L. Bobo (Eds.), *Racialized politics*. Chicago: University of Chicago Press.

Bobo, L., Kluegel, J.R., and Smith, R.A. (1997). <u>Laissez-Faire Racism: The Crystallization of a Kinder, Gentler, Antiblack Ideology</u>. In Steven A. Tuch and Jack K. Martin, eds., Racial attitudes in the 1990s: Continuity and Change, pp. 15-42. Westport CT: Praeger.

Bradley, M. (1991). The Iceman Inheritance: Prehistoric Sources of Western Man's Racism, Sexism and Aggression. New York, NY: Kayode Publications, LTD

Brewer, M. B. (2001) Ingroup Identification and Intergroup Conflict: When does Ingroup Love Become Outgroup Hate? In R. D. Ashmore &; L. Jussim (Eds), Social identity, intergroup conflict, and conflict reduction: Rutgers series on self and social identity; vol. 3. (pp. 17-41). London, England: Oxford University Press.

Brewer, M. B., and Campbell, D. T. (1976). <u>Ethnocentrism and Intergroup Attitudes</u>. New York, Wiley.

Brewer, M. B. and Brown, R. (1998). <u>Intergroup Relations</u>. In D.T. Gilbert, S.T., Fiske, and G. Lindzey (Eds.), The Handbook of Social psychology (4th ed., Vol. 2, pp. 554-594). New York: McGraw-Hill.

Brink, W. And Harris, L. (1967). <u>Black and White</u>. New York: Simon and Schuster.

Campbell, D. T., and LeVine, R. A. (1968). <u>Ethnocentrism and intergroup relations</u>. In R. Abelson and others (Eds.), Theories of cognitive consistency. A sourcebook. Chicago: Rand McNally

Coon, C.S. (1968). The Origins of Races. New York: Alfred A. Knopf

Darwin, C. (2009).   <u>The Origin of Species.</u> ALACHUA, FL: Bridge-Logo

Darwin, C. (1998). <u>The Descent of Man</u>. New York: Prometheus Books

DeGruy, J. (2020). 2011 Building Bridges – Keynote. Alabama State University. Lecture [Online] Available. https://www.youtube.com/watch?v= pact4iJLlog

DeGruy, J. (2020). <u>Black History Convocation 2020 with Dr. Joy DeGruy</u>. Alabama State University. Lecture [Online] Available. https://www.youtube.com/ watch?v=pact4iJLlog

Dovidio, J. F. and Gaertner, S. L. (Eds.). (1986). <u>Prejudice,</u>

Discrimination, and Racism. New York: Academic Press.

Feagin, J.R. and Feagin, C.B. (1996). Racial and Ethnic Relations. (2 ed.). Englewood Cliffs, NJ: Prentice Hall.

Fiske, S. (1998). Stereotyping, Prejudice, and Discrimination. In D. T. Gilbert, S. T. Jones, J. M. (1996). Prejudice and Racism. (2nd Ed.) Columbus, OH: McGraw-Hill.

Katz, I., Wackenhut, J., and Hass, R. G. (1986). Racial Ambivalence, Value Duality, and Behavior. In J. F. Dovidio and S. L. Gaertner (Eds.), Prejudice, Discrimination, and Racism. New York: Academic Press.

McGuire, B. C. (2019). The Ignoble Paradox of Man. (Revised Ed.) Kindle Direct Publishing, Indie Publishing. [Online] Available: www.amazon.com

McGuire, B. C. (2020). The Color of Our Souls. Kindle Direct Publishing, Indie Publishing. [Online] Available: www.amazon.com

McGuire, B. C. (2020). The Great Divide: The Social and Cultural Context of Inequality. (First Ed.) Kindle Direct Publishing. Indie Publishing. [Online] Available: www.amazon.com

McGuire, B. C. (2021). Refusing to Learn: Really, How

Dumb Do You Think I Am? (First Ed.) Kindle Direct Publishing. Indie Publishing. [Online] Available: www.amazon.com

McGuire, B. C. (2021). Racism: In the Behavioral Context of Intergroup Conflict and Hostility. (First Ed.) Kindle Direct Publishing. Indie Publishing. [Online] Available: www.amazon.com

Rothman, R. A. (1999). Inequality and Stratification: Race, Class, and Gender. (3rd Ed.). Upper Saddle River, New Jersey: Prentice Hall.

Schaefer, R. T. (2005). Race and Ethnicity in the United States. (3rd Ed.). Upper Saddle River, New Jersey: Prentice Hall.

Sears, D. O. (1987). Symbolic Racism. In P. Kitz & D. Taylor (Eds.), Towards the Elimination of Racism: Profile in Controversy. New York: Plenum.